W

Have you ever thought what a watery planet we live on? Seventy-one per cent of the world's surface is sea, and we're surrounded by it. And what's more, all around us there are countless lakes, ponds, rivers and streams – not to mention man-made waterways like canals.

Hundreds of different kinds of animals – birds, mammals, insects, amphibians and even reptiles – live in, on or near this water, and in *Water Watch* Dick King-Smith tells you what to look out for and where you'll be most likely to see it. There are so many animals to learn about: sea creatures (from shellfish and crabs at the seaside, to puffins and even seals near rocky coastlines); river creatures (read about the amazing 5,600 mile journey the eel makes, through fresh and salt water, in order to breed); lake and marshland creatures (have fun identifying the different water-birds – a pair of binoculars might come in handy!); local village or garden pond creatures (would you recognize a Great Crested Newt if you met one?); and there's even a chapter on the Loch Ness monster (decide for yourself whether it really exists).

Water Watch is crammed with fascinating information and stories about the many water creatures Dick King-Smith has observed and met – keep this book handy, and one day you'll have your own animal stories to tell. Happy animal-watching!

Dick King-Smith was a farmer in Gloucestershire for many years and this background has proved invaluable for his amusing animal stories. He also taught in a village primary school but he now writes full time. He has more recently become well-known for his television appearances with his miniature wire-haired dachshund, Dodo, on TV-am's *Rub-a-Dub-Tub* programme.

Dick King-Smith

WATER WATCH

Discover the creatures that live in, on or near water

Illustrated by Catherine Bradbury

PUFFIN BOOKS

PUFFIN BOOKS

Published by the Penguin Group
27 Wrights Lane, London w8 5 tz, England
Viking Penguin Inc., 40 West 23rd Street, New York, New York 10010, USA
Penguin Books Australia Ltd, Ringwood, Victoria, Australia
Penguin Books Canada Ltd, 2801 John Street, Markham, Ontario, Canada l3r1b4
Penguin Books (NZ) Ltd, 182–190 Wairau Road, Auckland 10, New Zealand

Penguin Books Ltd, Registered Offices: Harmondsworth, Middlesex, England

First published 1988

Made and printed in Great Britain by
Cox and Wyman Ltd, Reading, Berks
Filmset in Linotron Baskerville by
Rowland Phototypesetting Ltd, Bury St Edmunds, Suffolk

CONTENTS

Chapter 1

WATER, WATER EVERYWHERE

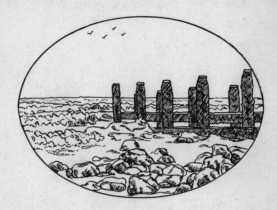

Have you ever thought what a watery planet we live on?

Look at a globe, or a map of the world, and you'll see great lumps of land like Africa or the Americas, but they're all just big islands in the enormous oceans. Seventy-one per cent of the world's surface is sea, and we, in our little British Isles, are surrounded by it.

Also, because our country is in a temperate zone and the rainfall's quite high, its counties are mottled with ponds and lakes and veined with streams and rivers. And near all that fresh and salt water, or over it, or on it, or in it, lives a host of animals.

This book is about a few of the interesting

creatures who need, in one way or another, to live their lives in watery surroundings.

Let's begin by going to one of my favourite places.

Let's go to the seaside.

Chapter 2

BY THE SEA

Going to the seaside means different things to different people. For me as a boy it meant (and still means) going to Tenby in Pembrokeshire, in west Wales. Nowadays Pembrokeshire is part of a new county called Dyfed, but I'm stuffy and stubborn and like to stick to the old name.

One of my great-uncles happened upon Tenby in the 1890s and liked the look of the place, so for the next sixty years or so all the different branches of my family followed his example, every summer.

My mother and father actually met there. He was walking on the pier (with two sticks – he had been badly wounded in the Great War, as I was destined to be in the next one, twenty-two years later) when he saw this pretty girl. Later, hobbling across the sands, he looked up and saw her leaning out of a window – like Juliet – of a house situated on the cliffs high above. (He had found out where she was staying, and that she was confined to her room with a cold.)

HOPE YOU ARE BETTER SOON

he wrote in the sand with one of his sticks.

So seaside meant Tenby and Tenby meant the Pembrokeshire coast and its great granite cliffs against whose feet the Atlantic rollers came crashing, all the way from America. And beneath and above and on the rocky faces of those cliffs were a million sea-birds.

Being on holiday meant waking (early, because so excited) on the first morning and hearing, on the roof above and from all the other roofs of the town, the voices of the Herring-gulls.

Some whined like peevish children, some barked like dogs, some mewed like cats, and some seemed to laugh madly while others made a quick, low, anxious 'qua qua qua'. Mostly they cried 'Kee-ow kee-ow kee-owk owk owk!' and I have only to hear this call – as often I can when gulls fly past my study window on their way to some new-turned ploughing – to be back in Pembrokeshire, a hundred miles and more away.

Beneath the upstairs window of the sitting-room in the house where we always stayed in Tenby was a garden wall. Normally no birds sat on it, probably because it was cat country, but every morning just before breakfast a crowd of Herring-gulls would arrive to sit along the wall in a row, cat-calling and chuckling and kee-owing, watching the window with their cold yellow eyes. They knew the routine, which never varied.

Every morning, just before breakfast, I walked with my father and my brother (and, later, with my own children) to the shop of Mr Raines the baker – a huge, bald, floury man with a dusty white apron that came down to his boots – to buy fresh rolls. They were hot from the oven and crusty, and the smell of them was heaven. Everyone saved some of the doughy middle of their rolls and kneaded it into bread-pellets. Then, at the end of the meal, the window was opened and the gulls came flocking.

Screaming and yelling, they fought for a place on the window-sill, battering one another and the glass with their powerful wings, while others dived and twisted for pellets thrown up into the air, till all was gone. Then the window was closed and the top of the wall was bare once more.

When you are at the seaside and you look at gulls, swimming in the sea or walking on the sands or flying around the cliffs, don't just think 'sea-gulls'. It's much more fun to try to identify them.

As well as the Herring-gull, there are five other main species living around the coast (and on the fields and in the towns and round the rubbish heaps) of Great Britain. There is the Black-headed Gull, the Common Gull, the Great Black-backed Gull, the Lesser Black-backed Gull and the Kittiwake.

Just to confuse things, the Herring-gull doesn't only eat herrings but anything and everything else it can find; the Lesser Black-backed has a grey back; the Black-headed Gull's head isn't black but dark chocolate, except in winter when the chocolate colour is lost, leaving only a dark smudge to the rear of the eye, so that the bird looks quite different and is then sometimes mistaken for the Common Gull, which isn't particularly common!

Let me try and sort things out for you.

The Herring-gull is a biggish bird with a heavy bill that has a red spot on its lower part. (The red spot, it is thought, acts as a kind of target or lure for the nestlings to peck towards, causing the parent to

great black-backed gull

herring-gull

common gull

disgorge food for them.) It has flesh-coloured legs and its plumage is grey-and-white. However it doesn't turn that colour until its fourth year: young Herring-gulls have mottled brown plumage, and so, incidentally, do immature Lesser Blackbacks which makes identification tricky. But the adult Lesser Blackback, similar in size to a smallish Herring-gull, has a much darker-grey back than the latter, and yellowish legs.

The Great Black-backed Gull you can't mistake. It's a lot bigger than the other native gulls, its back is really black, its legs are pinkish, and its head and bill appear heavy. The Great Blackback is a mighty predator, killing and eating mammals, young gulls or weak adult gulls. Everything about it looks threatening – its appearance, its walk (which is more of a waddle), and even its voice, a deep 'Aw-aw!'

Between Herring-gulls and Common Gulls there are obvious differences. The Common Gull is smaller, the head more delicate, and the beak slenderer, with no red spot on it. The legs are greenish-yellow, and when the bird is resting the wings protrude beyond the tail, which gives it a tapering appearance. It's nothing like as widespread as the Herring-gull and indeed breeds mainly in the Scottish Highlands.

Black-headed Gulls are two-a-penny, elegant birds with blood-red bills and legs, and, like the Herring-gulls, they come inland a great deal and are great frequenters of rubbish dumps. They're also very nimble fliers, able to skim over water and, barely touching the surface, seize food in their beaks. This is specially useful to them because they can keep their plumage clean in one of their favourite haunts – the sewage farm.

The last of our six truly native species of gull is the Kittiwake, another bird which, like the peewit and the cuckoo, gets its name from its cry – a shrill 'Kittee-waak!' (It also does a very good imitation of a baby crying.) No other gull is found so far out to sea, and indeed the Kittiwake, actually the most numerous of all our gulls, is an essentially maritime bird, only coming to land to breed. Like other sea-birds, Kittiwakes can drink sea-water and convert it into fresh in their bodies. Smaller and daintier than the Common Gull, they also have different-coloured legs – black ones. Kittiwakes are cliff-breeders, making their nests on ledges, as do many other sea-birds.

As Great Britain is an island, with a long, indented shoreline with cliff-faces and lots of little islets ('private' havens from man and other predators), and also because the warm waters of the

kittiwake

Gulf Stream provide plentiful small fish, twenty-four species of sea-bird actually breed here.

The numbers of all of them are increasing, except for the members of the auk family – the Puffins, the Razorbills and the Guillemots. All these, because they dive down from the surface for fish, are more liable than others both to becoming entangled and drowned in the nylon nets that modern trawlers use, and to oil pollution.

Oil pollution is a terrible hazard for sea-birds. Two things happen once a bird is contaminated with oil. First, it loses buoyancy and can simply drown. Secondly, the insulation that its feathers normally provides is lost, and the bird may die of cold. Furthermore, the natural reaction of a contaminated sea-bird is to try to clean itself and, in doing this, it actually swallows some of the oil, and this of course is fatal.

The care of oil-polluted birds is really a job for experts, and there are centres around the country where this can be done properly.

First, it needs two people to wash an oiled bird – one to hold, one to soap. Then all the detergent must be washed thoroughly out of the feathers, which often takes a good hour. And lastly, the cleaned bird has to be carefully fed, first with glucose and then with small bits of fish, for up to two weeks, before it's fit to be returned to the sea.

The strangest-looking member of the auk family is without doubt the Puffin. Everything about it is comical (just look at the drawing of it on the spine of this book!), and a famous Pembrokeshire naturalist described it perfectly as 'exactly like a mechanical duck with a parrot's head'.

Of all the sea-birds that you may come across, the Puffin is the most unmistakable. If you can't tell a Puffin from the rest, then you'd probably muddle a giraffe with an elephant. Partly it's because of its shape – thickset and stumpy, and its

puffin

colouring – black-and-white with bright orange
feet; but mostly it's on account of its beak, a
whopping great triangular thing, striped with
grey-blue, scarlet and yellow. It can carry an
astonishing number of small fish in it, which it
catches by diving under the surface of the water
and swimming with its wings like a penguin. To
add to its clown-like appearance, even the Puffin's
flight is a droll sight as it whirrs along like a

wound-up toy; and, to top it all, it usually nests in rabbit burrows.

Though its beak is nothing like as dramatic as the Puffin's, the Razorbill's is distinctive, as its name implies, and makes it easy to distinguish

razorbill

guillemot

from the third member of the auk family, the Guillemot.

Razorbills are also sturdy black-and-white birds, with a thickset, flattened bill which has a distinctive white grooved line across the middle. The Guillemot's plumage is a very dark brown-and-white, and it's a slenderer and more penguin-like bird.

The Razorbill typically swims with its tail cocked up, and dives for fish from the surface, as does the Guillemot which again uses its wings underwater. Both species fly fast and low over the waves, and the young of both Razorbill and Guillemot leave their nests for the sea at two-and-a-half weeks, long before they can actually fly. If you want to catch out someone who thinks they know all about British birds, ask them which is the most numerous sea-bird. They'll probably say 'gull'. The answer is 'guillemot'.

Unlike the gulls, the auk family are not particularly good at getting about on their flat feet, being clumsy movers on land, to say the least. But there is one sea-bird whose feet are set so far back on its body that it can only manage a drunken shuffle.

This is the Manx Shearwater, so called as it once bred in large numbers on the Isle of Man, and because when flying at sea (black-feathered above and white below) it skims low over the water, following the rise and fall of the swell, and continually 'shears' on one wing-tip, turning its body to show the black-and-white alternately. It is a

manx shearwater near burrow

bird designed for a highly specialized life in the air or on the sea, but *not* on the land.

The Manx Shearwater's domestic life is extraordinary. In April the female lays a single egg, underground in a shallow burrow or again an old rabbit-hole, to be safe from predatory gulls; then straight away off she flies to the Bay of Biscay (a mere five or six hundred miles away) to build up her strength on sardines, before flying back home. All this time the poor old male is sitting on the egg in the burrow, not having eaten a single mouthful of food, until his mate returns to relieve him.

Predators to rival the Great Blackbacks are the Great Skuas, or 'bonxies' as they're sometimes called, which not only take eggs and chicks but also

great skua

kill other smaller sea-birds. In addition bonxies are very aggressive towards humans who come into their territories, diving down to strike at the nearest bit, the top of the head. It pays to wear a hat, specially (tell your grandad, or your dad if the cap fits) should the top of the head be bald!

Another little trick that the dark and powerful

Great Skua has is to chase another much larger sea-bird, the gannet, and harass it until it disgorges its cropful of fish, thus providing the bonxie with a free meal.

The gannet is a magnificent and spectacular bird, a cigar-shaped giant with narrow wings that span a full six feet. Its habitat is the open sea, but it comes ashore to breed, often in large, packed colonies. 150,000 pairs is the estimate of British gannet numbers, and their choice of sites is upon cliffs and rocky islands and 'stacks' (isolated pillars of rock rising out of the sea – common in Pembrokeshire, for example). Usually just one egg is laid in a nest of seaweed and other vegetation, and both adults incubate.

But the fantastic thing about the gannet is the way in which it plunge-dives to catch fish, not – as the auks do – from the surface, but from a height of seldom less than ten metres (thirty-two feet) and often from as high as thirty metres, or about a hundred feet. Imagine yourself (but only imagine) diving from a hundred-foot-high cliff to hit the water with your nose. Goodbye, reader – it was nice knowing you.

But the gannet has a specially adapted skull, and air-sacs under its skin, and its nostrils are concealed and protected in its unique steel-grey

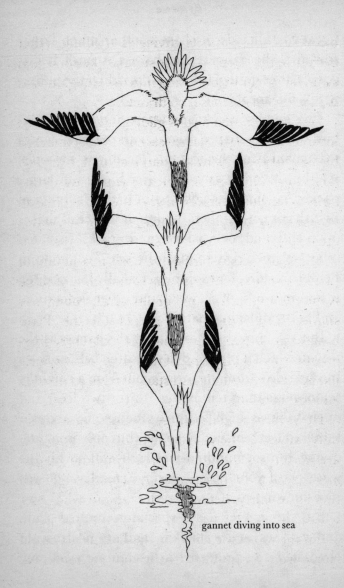

gannet diving into sea

bill. Watching gannets diving is thrilling. After each dive they pop up to the surface like corks and swim for a little before rising into the air again. But it's the dive itself that is so dramatic.

One moment the bird is gliding high in the sky, looking startlingly white except for its marked black wing-tips, its head bent, looking for the fish far below. The next instant the wings are closed tight to the body and down goes the gannet like an arrow, almost vertically, lancing into the sea with a great splash.

Many of the sea-birds I've been talking about (and I've only mentioned the commonest of those twenty-four species) live or breed all round our shores. The reason I've picked on the Pembrokeshire coast as an example of a breeding-ground is not simply out of nostalgia, but because its spectacular islands and stacks and cliffs provide an ideal habitat.

However, the different types don't nest willy-nilly, any old where. Herring-gulls, for example, are not great cliff-nesters, preferring low ground and indeed buildings as sites. And on the cliff itself there's a fairly definite order about who goes where.

On the top of the cliffs are the Puffins. (The old Norse word for 'puffin', by the way, is 'lundi'. No

prizes for guessing who were the first bird inhabi-
tants of that island in the middle of the Bristol
Channel.) And also on the top storey are the
shearwaters.

Next highest are the gannets on their big nests of
seaweed. Below them, the Kittiwakes build their
large, straggly structures on the most precarious
ledges, sometimes no more than six inches (sixteen
centimetres) wide.

Below the Kittiwakes, on the lower part of the
cliff, is Guillemot and Razorbill territory, the
Razorbills laying in deep crevices, and the Guillemots laying directly on to the rock of flat narrow
ledges. Sensible Razorbills, you might think, their
egg won't fall off the cliff. Silly Guillemots, theirs
will. Well, no doubt it sometimes does, but in fact
the Guillemot's egg is very cunningly shaped,
being much more pointed at one end, so that if it is
nudged it spins round and round instead of
toppling over.

Beneath the cliffs of course is the shoreline, and
here are many other birds, quite distinct in looks
and habits from those of the cliffs. Generally these
are called 'waders' or 'shore-birds' (neither name
particularly apt because they often nest in open
ground far from water), and there are many, many
different kinds, some of which I'll tell you about in

oyster-catcher and mussels

a later chapter. Just for now I want to mention only one – perhaps the most typical and certainly one of the showiest – the Oyster-catcher.

It's an unmistakable bird, large, black-and-white, with pink legs and, most noticeably, a long, orange-red bill. Using this, it eats its own weight of mudworms and shellfish every day. In past centuries, when they were much more common, the shellfish that gave the bird its name must have been on the menu, but now the main item is the mussel.

Following the ebbing tide as it reveals all this food, the Oyster-catcher either stabs the mussel open or smashes its shell, and the youngsters watch and imitate. It's a very noisy bird, with two main calls (both loud), a 'Kleep kleep!' and a 'Pic pic pic!' Also it has a sort of song, a loud (you guessed), accelerating trill.

Lastly – between the cliff-birds and the shore-birds – lives a bird that's usually as silent as the Oyster-catcher is noisy (though at breeding time there's a lot of growling and croaking in the colonies in which it lives), the cormorant.

> The Common Cormorant or Shag
> Lays eggs inside a paper bag.
> The reason you will see, no doubt –
> It is to keep the lightning out.
> But what these unobservant birds
> Have never noticed is that herds
> Of wandering bears may come with buns
> And steal the bags to hold the crumbs.

Christopher Isherwood wasn't quite as good a naturalist as he was a poet, because in fact the shag is a different bird, slightly smaller than the cormorant and greenish-tinged, with wings less square-edged and with a rapider beat.

The cormorant itself is a large, heavily built bird, an expert swimmer and a strong flier. Mostly it fishes from the surface, either by first making a

cormorant

distinct jump clear of the water or by submerging with barely a ripple. It works the shallow, inshore waters, catching mostly flat-fish.

Let's leave the seaside for the time being (we'll come back) with a typical sight in mind – a cormorant standing on a rock or buoy, with its wings outspread. No one seems to be absolutely certain why it does this. To relax certain muscles? To help digestion? Generally, it's thought that the bird is drying its feathers. But why should it need

29

to do that? Why hasn't it waterproof plumage like other water-birds? Who can tell? Only a cormorant, I suppose.

Chapter 3

BY THE RIVER

The word 'river' means a large stream of water. For smaller flows we use a variety of words – 'stream' itself, 'brook', 'beck' in the North, 'gill' and 'burn' in Scotland (once 'bourne' – think of all the names of English towns and villages ending with that). But all these words refer as a rule to tributaries or feeders which end their courses by joining a proper river. And of course the river itself starts small.

Many of our rivers flow through two quite separate types of landscape on their way to the sea. Each river starts in the uplands as a troutbeck, fast, cold, with lots of dissolved oxygen to aerate it, but probably low in mineral content. If it runs over peaty moorland, the water will be rather acid. Often the troutbeck will run at first over solid rock, stones and boulders. Only in deep eddies, or where some obstruction makes the flow change course, will there be any gravel or silt, allowing plants to root. This clean, bubbly water is ideal for trout, who feed by sight on insects, principally the young, aquatic stages of mayflies, stoneflies and caddis-flies.

Then, often, the river begins to change. Leaving the uplands – perhaps when the first cornfields come into sight – the river begins to run more slowly across flatter, richer country. Minerals and salts will be washed in from the bordering fields or brought in by tributaries, and the river water will have become warmer with less oxygen; it will be more fertile too, with plenty of rich silt at the bottom and thus a mass of water-plants. Here coarse fish like perch, roach, rudd, chub, carp and bream, which often feed by smell rather than by sight, are plentiful, taking the place of the trout in these murkier waters.

Not all British rivers follow this two-part journey. In the south and east, for example, there are very few upland sections of rivers, and in the hilly west, some rivers have no lowland stretch but dash from the mountains straight to the sea.

Many of the slow-flowing, flatland rivers run through clay, but in certain parts – Hampshire and Wiltshire, for example – chalk-streams are the rule. (Many of these are sizeable rivers but they're usually all called chalk-streams.) Their character is quite different from that of clay rivers. Their waters are full of calcium carbonate dissolved from the chalk and so run clear and 'hard'. (It's difficult to make soap lather well in 'hard' water: easy in 'soft' troutbeck water.) They also have a fairly even temperature – relatively warm in winter – so that waterside plants bloom early.

Chalk is a porous rock and the rain soaks down into it until it meets watertight rock, and then a spring gushes up and a chalk-stream begins. Some flow only in winter, when the chalk has soaked up enough of the autumn rains, and these are called 'winterbournes'.

Chalk-streams have no high banks, so are not suited to creatures like otters or kingfishers, but two animals that are found in them are crayfish (a kind of miniature lobster, to which it is related), and a nice little fish called the bullhead or Miller's Thumb.

Different types of river suit different fish, though sadly some rivers have become so polluted by chemical waste and other man-caused effluents that fish cannot exist: the lower reaches of the Thames became very foul, but things have improved now and indeed salmon have returned there.

The salmon, I imagine, would be top of the pops for the true fisherman, and the trout second. Anglers class these as game fish.

My experience of trout-fishing is limited. A friend once took me out in a boat to the middle of a lake, and we both sat there, fishing. It was a very hot, glaring sort of day (not good for fishing). He taught me to cast, that is to use the rod to throw out a length of line so that the artificial fly would drop – very gently – at the right spot on the water. I practised casting. Time passed. I got quite good at casting. It got hotter. Nothing stirred. We sat there for nine hours. I caught nothing. He caught nothing. We went home. I haven't fished since.

Our native trout is the Brown Trout. Ideally it likes fast rivers but slow ones will do providing there's enough oxygen – as in a chalk-stream. Brown Trout swim up to the head of the river – to the troutbeck – to spawn (to lay their eggs). Though they like cold water and can live in water from 0 to 25°C, they grow fastest in water between 7 and 19°C.

Spawning is triggered by a drop in water

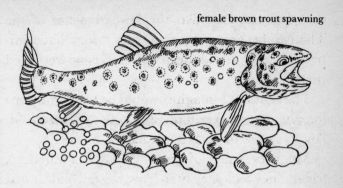

female brown trout spawning

temperature to 6°C, so it's therefore something that takes place in autumn and winter. For a spawning-ground trout need a clean gravel bottom that's washed by running water. The eggs are laid in great quantities, but mortality among the small fry (babies) is very high, and out of hundreds maybe only a single pair will survive to grow and breed.

The Brown Trout has an imported American relation, the Rainbow Trout, which lives in slower rivers and also in gravel pits and reservoirs. Brown Trout are mature at about four years, and they do not migrate to sea.

But the salmon feeds, develops and grows in the sea. Then it returns to the river to spawn, once again in gravelly spawning-grounds or 'redds' at the head of the river. Just as human beings have

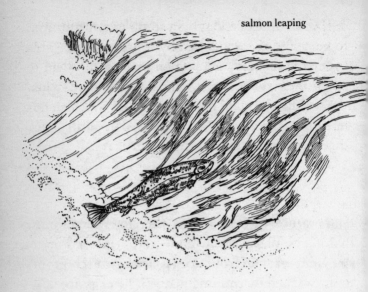

salmon leaping

three stages to get through – baby, girl, woman, or baby, boy, man – so the salmon goes under a variety of names depending on its age.

Once hatched, the babies are known as fry until they are finger-length. Then, for the remainder of their first two years, which they spend in the river of their birth, they are parr. The next year each goes to sea, as a smolt, growing fast in rich feeding-grounds off Greenland, and at the age of three becomes a grilse. The grilse then returns to its river to spawn, and after spawning goes back to sea as a grilse kelt. Only after all that is the fish known as a salmon.

If you're lucky enough, in summer and autumn, to be near a river spanned by weirs, you'll be able to see the magnificent salmon leaping up them to reach their spawning-grounds. Once there, when the hen-fish has laid her eggs and the cock-fish has fertilized them, the exhausted pair drift back downstream, and many die on the way.

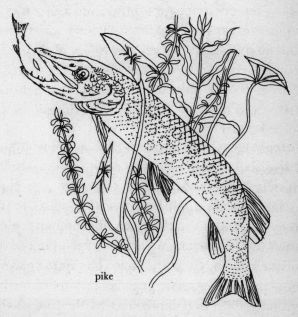

pike

If the salmon is the most majestic of British fish, the pike is the most awesome. It is the supreme predator, long-lived and capable of growing to a huge size (the largest of all in big lakes and lochs, where fish of fifty pounds weight [twenty-two kilo-grams] have been recorded). Young pike are called jacks and for their first year stay in the shallows, feeding on freshwater shrimps and other insects. But then they are soon about their murderous work, taking prey of about one eighth their own size, so that in late summer a five centimetre jack is killing one centimetre minnows; and as it grows, so it takes larger prey, including young water-birds. The method is the same, regardless of the age or size of the pike. As the lion kills after a short fast charge, so the pike makes a sudden lightning strike, and then the victim is turned head on and gulped down.

And they're not fussy about who gets gulped. There's a record of a twenty-three pound (ten kilogram) pike which, when caught, was found to have in its stomach one eighteen-inch pike plus two linen bags inscribed 'Wiltshire Saus-ages'.

And here's a bit of a poem called 'Pike' that the Poet Laureate, Ted Hughes, wrote.

Two, six pounds each, over two feet long,
High and dry and dead in the willow-herb –
One jammed past its gills down the other's gullet:
The outside eye stared . . .

38

I remember as a boy wading in a crystal-clear Wiltshire chalk-stream with my pants rolled up when suddenly a good-sized pike shot between my bare legs. In fact I suppose he was after some fish behind me, but it scared the pants off me.

One of the strangest fish to be found in our rivers is the eel. Its body gives the impression of a snake, but the eel is a fish, having a dorsal fin (a long fringe all down its back) and pectoral fins (corresponding to the forelimbs of higher animals) at the join of head and body. Also it breathes through gills and therefore can't survive indefinitely on land, though it can do so longer than almost all other fish. Indeed, when journeying to breed, it can make part of its trip from pond, stream or ditch to the sea by travelling overland for short distances if the grass is soaked with dew.

When it reaches the sea, it stays awhile in the estuary to get itself acclimatized, and then it makes a journey of no less than 5,600 kilometres across the Atlantic to the Sargasso Sea, between the Azores and the Bahamas. Here the eggs are laid and fertilized, and the adults die.

Next in this amazing saga the baby eels, known as elvers, make the return journey to our shores, arriving in vast numbers, numbers that are reduced by predators such as gulls and other birds,

lesser black-backed gull eating elvers

by adult eels, and by man. In the Severn Estuary, for example, great quantities of elvers are caught and transported to be kept and fed until they are big enough for the jellied-eel trade.

These are all Common Eels, not to be confused with a much larger marine cousin, the Conger Eel, which is sometimes found stranded on the shore and which can grow to seven feet (two metres) long and be as thick round as a man's thigh!

Common Eels are at first known as Yellow Eels, and if kept in inland waters (by accident or design) remain yellow and live to a good age. But for most a change occurs. They become Silver Eels, and swim back to the Sargasso to breed and die. Female eels are much bigger than the males (which seldom exceed seventeen inches [forty-five centimetres]). Eels' food is larvae, snails, fish, fish-eggs and each other.

Yellow Eels can live a very long time. There have been several specimens in Ireland known to have survived thirty years, and fifty years is not unknown. One, caught as an elver in 1863, died in 1948 – eighty-five years later!

Where there are fish there are fishers, and the most beautiful must be a bird that is brilliant blue-green above and chestnut below, with a white throat and neck-patch, and a vivid cobalt stripe up its back – the kingfisher.

The Greek name for kingfisher is *halcyon*, and the ancients believed that the birds laid their eggs in a nest on the surface of the sea and that for the two weeks of incubation the gods forbade the winds to blow – 'halcyon days' . . .

In fact, the kingfisher makes a tunnel in the river bank, and so it favours the kind of stream that has a steep, rat-proof bank, in which it digs a tunnel perhaps a metre long and lays its six to seven eggs in a hollowed-out nest-chamber at the end of it. It also needs bankside shrubs so that it can sit on a

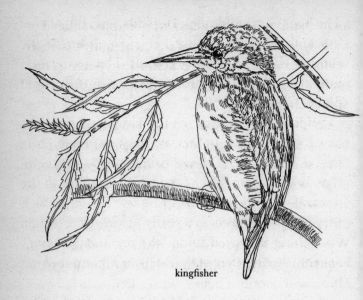

kingfisher

favourite perch, high enough above the water's surface to see its prey, from which it dives, though occasionally it will hover before plunging. Often it submerges to grasp its quarry. As well as small fish, the kingfisher catches tadpoles and aquatic invertebrates.

In shape the kingfisher is dumpy and big-headed, with a long dagger bill and a very short tail. But it's the brilliance of its colouring that is unforgettable when you see it skimming the surface of the river at high speed (and you have to be quick too – or it's gone before you can focus on it).

The poet Gerard Manley Hopkins used the phrase 'As kingfishers catch fire . . .', just right for the sudden flame of blazing colour. The bird has a little trilling song, but the usual note – in low rapid flight – is a piping 'chee!'

Seldom as you may see the kingfisher, just because of its speed, in fact as many as 9,000 pairs nest in Britain. Two things principally affect them. One is poisoning, from pesticides washed into the streams and then taken up by the fish on which they prey. The other is a really hard winter, when everything is locked under the ice and the kingfishers, though they may catch fire, cannot catch fish.

A quite different bird, which also 'fishes' in streams, though for aquatic insects and their larvae, is the dipper. And it does this in the most extraordinary way. It actually walks along the bed of the stream, feeding underwater in even the most turbulent conditions. In fact the dipper prefers such conditions, frequenting fast-flowing, rocky, upland streams; though it can be seen in canals and on the margins of lakes, and I have certainly watched a pair on a fairly placid river near my home (though admittedly they were hunting in a fast-moving stretch of it).

It used to be thought that the dipper – which can

swim, though not well, for its feet are not webbed –
managed its amazing walking-on-the-bottom trick
by grasping weeds with its feet, and it may be that
it does hold on to stones to anchor itself; but
probably it is chiefly the pressure of the river flow
against its back that holds its body under. Also, to
help it remain submerged, it moves its wings in
and out (though not fully stretched, as in flight).
When it stops flapping, it bobs up.

dipper 'walking-on-the-bottom'

Its actual flight is fast and direct with whirring
wings, like a wren's, and in fact it looks a bit like a
big tubby wren. The dipper's nest also is domed
like a wren's, and always built over water, often on

44

a ledge underneath a bridge. Dippers are never still, bobbing and bowing, curtsying and dipping (leading to its name, probably, though it does have another, more poetic one, the water ousel). If you should visit a swift rocky stream and see a tubby stumpy bird, a dark blackish-brown all over except for a white breast, standing on a rock and bouncing up and down as though it was on springs, that's the dipper. Keep watching and you'll see its fantastic underwater walk.

Ted Hughes wrote a good poem called simply 'An Otter'. Here's a bit of it.

Underwater eyes, an eel's
Oil of water body, neither fish nor beast is the otter:
Four-legged yet water-gifted, to outfish fish;
With webbed feet and long ruddering tail
And a round head like an old tomcat.

The first thing to say about this animal – and it's a sad thing – is that, unless you happen to live in the wilds of the north of Scotland, you're fairly unlikely to see one.

To some extent this was always true, for the otter is a nocturnal animal and shy of man; and even when it was much more plentiful, you'd have been more likely to hear its fluty whistle than to set eyes on it. Otter-hunters saw more of them by day, of course, and killed a fair number, but thankfully the otter is now a protected animal, and instead the otter-hounds now hunt the feral mink, that is those that have escaped from fur farms and bred in the wild.

But hunting was not the cause of the decline in the numbers of British otters that took place in the second part of this century. Pesticides like Dieldrin have played their part, affecting the fish that the otters ate, but now that most pesticides have been renounced it can be seen that one important factor, that of river engineering – cutting banks, clearing obstructions, straightening up awkward bends and generally 'tidying' a river course – has turned what were once otter highways into sterile corridors.

Because of this breaking up of the otterways, pockets of otters may survive but are out of touch with others of their kind, and therefore at risk without fresh breeding-stock. To be sure, people who care about the otter have tried to help by providing quiet lengths of river, and even artificial holts (the name for an otter's den), but there's no way of telling the animals about this.

Between 1977 and 1979, a comprehensive otter survey was carried out and all the major rivers in

England, Wales and Scotland were checked. Broadly, the results were that sightings in northern Scotland were frequent, and that there were still otters present in the rest of Scotland, in the North of England, in Wales, in the south-west peninsula and in Norfolk. Elsewhere the score read: Otters – 0.

Otters (like badgers) are large members of the weasel family. They are fish-eaters but are specially fond of eels and frogs. They are nomadic, hunting one stretch for a while before moving on, and have a number of holts up and down their territories. A territory may include many rivers, and the otter may use the principal one as a main road, and lie up in the tributaries. Dog (male) otters move vast distances even in one night, but the bitch keeps nearer a particular home and she and her cubs have much smaller feeding-areas.

In general, otters tend to feed more in slower waters where the fish are bigger, and they mark their territories with tarry-looking droppings called 'spraints' (full of fish bones and, strangely, quite nice-smelling).

Otters have lovely natures. They are loyal (one will come to the aid of a wounded companion), brave and devoted to one another; and above all

otter family

they are playful animals, enjoying happy games with stones and other objects, and like to make and use slides, down banks and especially in the snow, down which they whizz endlessly with much noise and obvious grinning enjoyment.

But, above all, they are designed for water life. The rudder (tail) is used for changing direction when swimming, each foot has five widely splayed toes with webs between, and in pursuit of fish they are lightning-fast and tremendously acrobatic. They can swim under water without surfacing for three to four minutes, but a string of rising bubbles betray their presence, as the otter-hunters well knew.

On land, incidentally, the tail is used as a tripod or third leg to support the animal when standing upright to look around. The outer coat is harsh, with long guard hairs, and the undercoat is dense and, of course, waterproof.

The otter's whiskers are very sensitive, its sight and sense of smell excellent, and its bite a very nasty one. It's a heavy feeder, eating one third of its own body-weight every day. Dog otters usually weigh between twenty and twenty-five pounds (bitches four or five pounds less), so you can see that they put away lots of grub. As well as eels, frogs and fish, otters eat rats, mice and rabbits,

and will take ducklings too; and they can visit the
coast for a change of diet – seafood.

Generally their routine is controlled by the
habits of fish. When in late autumn fish go upstream to spawn, otters follow. Then in spring they
follow the new-born fish downstream.

Up to three cubs are born in the holt which may
well have an underwater entrance (to mask the
animals' scent). But the cubs, like you, have to be
taught to swim, and, like some of you, make an
awful fuss about it at first until they get the hang of
it and realize what fun it is. Here are a couple of
bits from what I think is the best animal story ever
written – *Tarka the Otter* by Henry Williamson. The
cub Tarka is just learning to swim.

When he went into the water the next night
and tried to walk towards his mother, he
floated. He was so pleased that he set out
across the river by himself, finding that he
could turn easily towards his mother by
swinging his hindquarters and rudder. He
turned and turned many times in his
happiness . . .

And a little later:

Tarka became excited and, seeing a fish, he
swam after it and went underwater to get it.

In order to travel faster, he struck out with all four webs together, and lo! Tarka was swimming like an otter near a fish. It was the biggest fish he had seen, and although he kicked after it at the rate of nearly two hundred kicks a minute, he lost it after a yard. He yikkered in his anger, and oh! Tarka was no longer swimming like an otter, but gasping and coughing on the surface, a poor little sick-feeling cub mewing for his mother.

Another good swimmer (though not in the otter's class) is the water vole. Some people wrongly call them water-rats (although no such animal exists), and this name clings on partly, I suspect, because of the character of Rat in that evergreen book, *The Wind in the Willows*. The author was thinking of a water vole, but the illustrator (at any rate in my old edition of 1927) drew Mole's friend as very rat-like, with a long pointed muzzle, large ears and a long naked tail.

The water vole does have a rather longer tail, as a swimming aid, than its land-based vole cousins, but like them it is blunt-nosed, with barely visible ears (which have a kind of lid to keep out water).

Your ears may be the first sense to tell you of a water vole's presence – 'plop' it goes as it dives.

water vole

Wait quietly and you'll see it swimming along, pushing a little ream of water before it, unless, that is, it has dived to reach the safety of its home: a water vole's burrow in a river-bank may have many entrances, several of them under water.

Water voles are common wherever there is good bankside vegetation to provide both cover and food; the sides of slow inland rivers are an ideal habitat and, as grass is its main food, clues to its presence are little piles of grass stems and shoots stacked ready for eating, and a roughly cropped 'lawn' on a bank.

The water vole, which is active day and night, not only uses regular 'runs' but also has regular 'swims', keeping the same course each time, and diving to avoid pursuit. Also its territory is small, since it doesn't feed far from its burrow. Nor would you if you had a list of enemies like this: otters, stoats, weasels, brown rats, herons, owls, pike and large trout!

One comparative newcomer to our rivers and streams that, as a vegetarian, wouldn't bother the little native water vole, is a strange-looking import, the coypu. At first sight, the coypu looks a bit like a giant rat, and indeed that's how showmen once exhibited them. Roll up, roll up, and see the Terrible Giant Monster Sewer Rat!

In fact they are very large rodents (as big as a good-sized dog) from South America, first imported into Norfolk in 1929. The idea was to farm them for fur, because beneath their coarse outer coats lies a beautiful, soft, plushy undercoat, known in the fur trade as 'nutria'.

As with so many other imported species (grey squirrels, muskrat, mink) it was only a matter of time (1937, in fact) before enough managed to

coypu

escape to breed in the wild; and feral coypus became quite widespread, particularly in East Anglia, where they assumed pest proportions. It was estimated at one time that the cost of eradicating them from that district alone could cost five million pounds. They damage crops, particularly sugar-beet on which they feed, and also damage river-banks and drainage dykes.

The population explosion of coypus was not surprising when you consider that they have two to three litters per year, each of between three and eleven young. So one female might have as many as thirty offspring within twelve months. The latest position in East Anglia is that the coypu population has been enormously reduced, thanks to a planned programme of humane trapping. Indeed, it's just possible that the animal has been eradicated.

In appearance they look rather hump-backed, with blunt heads and unmistakable incisors (front teeth) which are very large and bright orange in colour (and can give a very nasty bite). The hind-feet are webbed – they are very good swimmers – and a strange but very sensible thing about the females is that their teats, instead of being on the belly, are placed high along the animals' sides so that the young can actually suckle while the mother is swimming on the surface. The coypu's tail is long and scaly and strong, and it's by this that you pick it up. I know because I've often done it but I don't recommend you to try. If you don't hold the animal correctly, those orange teeth can do terrible damage.

I know a bit about coypu because my father kept them, just before the last war. A stream near our home ran through a withy-bed, and large pens were built there, surrounded by tall fencing, the bottom of which sunk into the ground to prevent the animals escaping by burrowing underneath (though one or two did). The stream was diverted into several channels which were made to flow through the pens, so that the coypus had running water to swim in; and small ponds were dug, in the middle of which were little islands, each having a barrel sunk in it. Each barrel had holes cut in its sides into which were fitted large drainpipes, and each barrel had a lid. Wade to the island, take off the barrel-lid and look in, and there they would be, in a nice straw-filled artificial home – often with a litter of babies. Ideal, you might think, but the venture came to nothing, all because of a minute worm called the liver-fluke.

My father bought a dozen or so animals to begin with, and they settled in well and bred happily. Time passed and the numbers grew, to seventy or eighty, and my mother had her sights on a fur coat. Then the coypu began to sicken and die, and no one knew why.

Eventually the reason was found. Sheep, in the riverside fields higher upstream, had been suffering from liver-rot which is caused by a fluke or worm, and the fluke, carried in the water, had been killing the coypu.

I don't remember that we ever sold any of the pelts commercially, though in the end there were just enough to make my mother's fur coat. But even that can't have been exactly top-quality, as I found out after her death, forty years later. I took the coat to a furrier and asked how much he would offer me for it.

He looked at it.

'Nutria!' I said proudly.

'Squirrel,' he said drily.

'But it was made from our own animals!' I spluttered. 'From our own coypu, that we bred!'

'Not this coat,' said the furrier. 'This is squirrel.'

At some point mother had swapped the second-rate coat for a better one.

By the way, if this story leads you to think that I approve of fur-farming, I don't. In those days I didn't give it a thought, but now I'm opposed to animals being exploited in this way. People should be satisfied with artificial furs. The real ones are meant to keep their owners warm.

I can't leave the river without a mention of the bird that is the very symbol of it – the swan.

We have three varieties of swan in these islands, and by far the commonest, the one we all know, is the Mute Swan.

The Whooper Swan, which is the same size, has a straighter neck and a bright yellow wedge at the side of its black bill. It breeds in far northern marshes.

Bewick's Swan is smaller and shorter-necked than the Whooper, and the yellow bill-patch is rounded, not wedge-shaped. Its breeding-grounds are in Siberia.

But the Mute Swan – which isn't mute, by the way (for it can hiss and snort), except in comparison with other swans – breeds in the British Isles. Orange-billed with a black knob at the beak's base, there are 5,000 pairs in Britain, but (and I'll come to this further on) those numbers are falling.

Don't approach a swan's nest, and don't go too near a pair with cygnets (babies). Both the cob (male) and the pen (female) will defend their young very aggressively, and a bang from a swan's big wing will break your arm just as efficiently as a sledge-hammer.

The cygnets, which when small sometimes ride on their mother's back as she swims, do not lose their brownish plumage and become fully white until they are over a year old. Then a strange thing happens. Their father, the cob, sees the colour white as meaning 'an intruder', and after having spent all his time defending his cygnets when they were brown, now takes to driving them fiercely away.

male swan and cygnets

The Mute Swan is one of the world's largest flying birds – an adult weighing over forty pounds (eighteen kilograms) – and they need a long stretch of water for take-off. In flight, the swan holds its neck out and the sound of its passage is unmistakable and thrilling. Legend has it that the swan sings before it dies, but the only 'singing' is the sound of those great wings beating.

But if the legend had been true, a great deal of swan-song would have been heard in recent years. Numbers are in decline, dramatically so on some rivers. For 400 years there has been a ceremony on the Thames below Reading called 'swan-upping', when the birds are counted. In 1956 there were 800 adults there and 200 cygnets. In 1984 there were 200 adults and only thirty-two cygnets.

Both river engineering and the increased use of pleasure boats have contributed to the decrease, but much the worst hazard is lead-poisoning.

It's simple. Swans are bottom feeders, reaching down with their long necks, and as well as water-plants they take up gravel to help them grind their food. Amongst the gravel are shotgun pellets and, much more commonly, lead angling-weights. The lead is worn down in the bird's gizzard and poisons it. Listlessness is one symptom of approaching death, and a characteristic kink in the drooped-back neck.

Unless fishermen can be persuaded to use other putty-like materials as weights, the large flocks of swans we are used to seeing, especially in or near towns where angling is more common, will become a thing of the past. A sad day that will be.

Chapter 4

IN THE WETLANDS

Earlier, I mentioned the waders, birds of the seashore and the saltings, which, because of Britain's favourable coastline, occur in enormous numbers. Many of them actually nest on the moors, and move back to the estuaries in autumn when the moorland becomes cold and inhospitable.

There is a large number of species of wader, and I'll try to pick out a few, the commonest; so that should you find yourself looking at a host of birds, all wading, all probing in the sand or the mudflats with their beaks, you won't just think 'Ah! Waders', but may be able to distinguish one sort from another.

Oyster-catchers are one, as I've mentioned, but the most numerous and widespread is the Dunlin, a round-shouldered, little brown bird that is also the smallest wader.

Huge numbers of Dunlins come here in winter from Russia, but quite a lot stay on and breed on our moors and by lakes and bogs in the Pennines, on Dartmoor and in Wales. The Dunlin has a long

dunlin

straight bill with which it probes for insects, molluscs, crustaceans and worms.

Another small wader is the Sanderling. As its name suggests, it keeps to sandy shores, and is very active; if you see a greyish bird racing along the beach in quick spurts and chasing the retreating waves, that'll be a Sanderling.

Much the same size, but browner and not as tubby, is the Common Sandpiper, and here (for it's quite difficult to tell some of these waders apart) you must listen for the piping 'Twee-see-see!' that gives it its name.

Names help. The Redshank, a slightly larger wader, has a red bill with a dark tip and red shanks (legs). No prizes for guessing a feature of the Greenshank. The Turnstone is so called because it has a short strong beak that it uses as a lever to turn over stones in search of insects and small shellfish; but the bill of the Bar-tailed Godwit is very long, allowing it to probe into deep mud.

The waders have bills of different lengths and shapes, to find food at various depths. Longest of all is the beak of the Curlew, which can find worms six inches (sixteen centimetres) down. The Curlew is the largest of the waders and perhaps the easiest to identify (apart from the unmistakable Oyster-catcher), partly by its bubbling, trilling 'Coorlee!' call, and partly by that very long and downward-curving bill.

Those are just some of the commoner waders, but with a good specialist reference book and a pair of binoculars, you may find many more.

curlew and young

One quite different species of bird commonly seen on estuary flats is the Shelduck, a brilliant creature with plumage of black/green, white and chestnut, with a scarlet bill that tips up a bit at the end like Donald Duck's. Shelduck are found all round Britain's coast (except where there are cliffs), and they feed on small snails in the muddy ooze, usually at ebb tide, following the receding water down and sifting the shells from the mud with a swinging action of their bills. They nest in

shelduck outside burrow

sand dunes and old rabbit burrows and even in holes in trees. The Shelduck is large, almost as big as the many types of geese that come down from the Arctic in wintertime to our estuaries and saltings.

The varieties include the 'grey' geese – the Greylag, the Pink-footed, the Bean and the White-front, and the 'black-necked' geese – the Brent and the Barnacle Goose. Barnacles are so called because in medieval times people thought that, just as tadpoles turn into frogs, so these particular birds began life as those shells that attach themselves by stalks to the bottom of a ship. They wrote of '. . . broken pieces of old ships on which is found certain spume or froth, which in time breedeth into shells, and the fish which is hatched therefrom is in shape and habit like a bird.'

Something not quite right there, methinks!

But the commonest goose is the Greylag, ancestor of our farmyard goose. The voice is much the same – a loud nasal honking. It's a big grey bird that breeds in marshes and on moorlands and the shores of lakes, and winters on pasture or arable land and on estuaries, feeding on grasses and farm crops.

Goose flight is very typical. When moving short distances, flocks may fly in an ill-defined 'gaggle', but for longer flights they form a V-shaped 'skein'. There are all sorts of aerodynamic theories for this, but the simple explanation is that a V is the obvious formation to keep together yet avoid flying directly behind the bird in front.

Geese also adopt a rather dramatic way of losing height quickly from a gliding position. This is called 'whiffling', and the bird sideslips, tips and twists to spill air; sometimes in fact, in the course of this manoeuvre, the bird's body is momentarily upside down though the head remains the right way up!

*

greylag goose

As well as our shores and the estuaries round the mouths of rivers, another important water habitat for wildlife is provided by the wetlands. Long ago, before they were drained for farmland, much of our lowlands were covered by the swamps and marshlands that then fringed the rivers.

Swamps are marked by reed-beds, which grow vigorously in shallow water, and can eventually rot down in the slow flow and form a firmish peaty soil, waterlogged for most of the year, known as a fen. Marshy land too is waterlogged, where streams ooze across pasture, or on heavy, ill-drained, clay bottoms. Wetlands is a term applied equally to swamp, marsh or damp meadowland, and the Somerset Levels, the Norfolk Broads and the Ouse Washes are examples of large wetland areas.

For a number of animals these watery conditions are ideal. Most are birds (though, of course, mammals like the otter, the water vole and the coypu could have swum about just as happily in this chapter as in the previous one), and some of these birds are particularly interesting.

One such is the Bittern, a large bird of the heron family. I can't promise you a sight of one because unfortunately they are rare and only hunt in thick cover, in the reed-beds of the Norfolk Broads. The decline in Bittern numbers is probably due to the continued disturbance of that habitat, but if you should be holidaying there you might hear it, even if you don't see it.

Its call is one of the strangest sounds in the bird world, a deep foghorn booming repeated three

bittern

to five times, which can be heard up to three miles away.

Even if you were to come upon one, you still might not see it, for the tawny-gold Bittern 'freezes', standing quite still (except that it actually sways in harmony with the reeds about it) with its neck stretched up so that its dagger bill points skywards. It hunts small mammals and frogs, negotiating even the softest mud on its long green toes; and it can actually move at different levels, by grasping a bunch of reeds with each foot in turn.

Other birds of the reed-beds are three sorts of warblers – the Sedge, the Reed and the Grass-hopper Warbler, and the Bearded Tit. If you hear a noise exactly like the squeal of a stuck pig, that's a Water Rail.

In the Washes of the Ouse lives another strange bird, the Ruff. In fact, Ruff is only the name of the male bird, for the females are called Reeves. The

male ruffs 'jousting'

males in springtime – you won't be surprised to hear – have a large, multi-coloured ruff of feathers around their necks and also feather 'eartufts'. But the remarkable thing about these birds is their courting display.

For all the world like knights of old, the Ruffs have 'tilting-grounds', traditional display areas on

harriers doing food pass

which the males 'joust' with one another. The
Reeves incidentally are smaller than the Ruffs, the
main exception to the general rule among waders.

Above the marsh you may see in flight one of the
less common of the raptors (birds of prey), the

harrier. There are three types of British harrier – the Marsh Harrier, Montagu's Harrier and the commonest, the Hen Harrier. A couple of hundred years ago harriers were almost wiped out, but they have made quite a good recovery. They feed on small mammals and birds (including ducklings), on reptiles, amphibians, large insects and worms. When the eggs are laid, the female incubates and the male hunts, and this leads to a fascinating piece of harrier behaviour, the food pass. As the male returns to the nesting-area with the prey, the female flies up to meet him and tips over on her back, and the food is actually passed from talon to talon.

In any marshy or boggy ground or by lake edges, you may surprise a brownish bird with a striped crown and a long bill. You'll be lucky to notice all that, because the Snipe, when disturbed, dashes away at high speed in a very distinctive zigzag flight, jinking from side to side. But its display flight is quite unique, for by spreading its outer tail feathers it produces a 'drumming' sound.

Probably the best known of all our waders is the Lapwing (or Peewit, or Green Plover, whatever you fancy). These are all names that tell you things.

Lapwing for flapwing – those slowish beats of its

rounded wings; Peewit for what it says; and finally Plover comes from the Latin word *pluvia* meaning 'rain' – the bird of wet places.

One last wader. I've left it till last, not just because it's a most elegant and beautiful bird, but because it was chosen as the emblem of the Royal Society for the Protection of Birds. It is the Avocet.

The reason for their choice must have had something to do with its looks (they would hardly have picked a dull, dumpy bird), but is mostly because the Avocet is the symbol of what man can do to help birds.

It was because of man's interference that the Avocet, which used to breed quite freely in Britain, disappeared from the face of these islands. For 100 years none bred anywhere in Britain or Ireland, until in 1938 a colony established itself briefly in county Wexford in south-east Ireland. Then, in 1947, four pairs were found breeding in Suffolk.

Now the success story begins. The RSPB established reserves on the Suffolk coast, where they managed the habitat very carefully to create the best conditions for nesting birds of many kinds, removing potential predators and protecting the birds from disturbance by humans.

To help the Avocets in particular, the RSPB artificially controlled the water levels in shallow

avocet

pools inside the sea walls, partly to give plenty of
shingle banks for nesting birds, but primarily to
give shallow water of the right salinity (saltiness)
for a plentiful supply of the Avocet's favourite food,
the brine shrimp.

The Avocet's appearance is dramatic. A tall
slender wader, black-and-white, with long, slate-
blue legs, it has an unmistakable upturned bill. Its
way of walking too is remarkable, a kind of ballet
movement, quick and graceful, lifting each foot to

the horizontal. In flight, its legs project backwards well beyond the tail, and it feeds in shallow water with a distinctive side-to-side sifting motion of that upcurved beak.

The story of the Avocet is an object lesson in conservation, showing how proper habitat management can create the best conditions, and give a sorely needed boost to a bird population that is in mortal danger. Man the destroyer *can* so easily become man the preserver.

You might like to join the RSPB. Membership gives you access to over sixty reserves in Great Britain and Northern Ireland, which include at least eighteen on the coast.

Let's leave the marshes, mudflats, swamps and saltings of Britain with a last look at a particular estuary. It's the Severn Estuary (not far from where I live), and on its eastern shore is a place called Slimbridge.

Here, in 1946, the famous ornithologist, Peter Scott, began the collection of waterfowl known as the Wildfowl Trust. By 1982 there were 3,000 birds at Slimbridge, 131 out of the 148 species of waterfowl in the world, occupying 1,100 acres of what Scott calls 'the longest bird-feeding-table in the world'.

Great things have been done here in the name of conservation, and perhaps the best-known example is the saving from extinction of the Hawaiian Goose or Ne-ne (so named from its soft call-note). In the late 1950s, there were only thirty-five Ne-ne left in the world. Three were brought to Slimbridge.

Now, after a careful and successful breeding programme, the world population is up to 1,000. What a nice story.

I've only met Peter Scott once. In about 1952, my wife and I went to Slimbridge with a young nephew, to see the swans and geese and ducks. It was early in the day and there were hardly any other members of the public in the pens, though I did see one man (whose face I recognized) looking at the birds. He was staring at a White-fronted Goose (at least I was pretty sure it was a White-fronted Goose), so I went up to him and said, 'Excuse me, is that a White-fronted Goose?' and he said, 'Yes, it is.'

Peter Scott explained that he was waiting for a guest whom he was going to show round; but while he was waiting (and that turned out to be a good hour), he showed the three of us round, pointing out all the different species and telling us interesting things about them. He couldn't have taken more trouble if we had been the long-awaited guest. (That turned out to be Prince Philip.)

Perhaps kindness to animals starts with kindness to people. What a nice man.

A familiar water-bird is the moorhen (whose name originates not from the moor, but from the mere),

moorhen and young

with its long greenish legs, red-and-yellow bill, and characteristic action, leaning forward as it runs, and continually jerking its head and tail when walking or swimming. Baby moorhens too are delightful fluffy things, and families that live near to a farm will often come in to feed with the poultry, so comparatively tame can they become. Moorhens in general prefer little ponds, avoiding large open waters, but a bird quite like them, the coot, flocks upon lakes in large numbers, unmistakable on account of the white bill and large white frontal shield above it, the origin, I suppose, of the expression 'as bald as a coot'.

Typically, the heron stalks slowly in the shallows, or stands motionless, waiting to stab with its long serrated bill. The flight too is unmistakable, the long legs trailing behind and the long neck drawn right back as the bird flaps in slow motion on big curved wings. Only yesterday one flew over the field called Burr Acre that I look at from my study window, twisting and turning clumsily in an effort to avoid a pair of carrion crows that were mobbing it, diving at the big bird in the hope that it would throw up its cropful of fish or eels from the nearby river and treat them to a free meal. In fact, though the heron's flight seems painfully slow, this is deceptive because it can do thirty m.p.h.

A heronry is a large collection of nests, untidy, precarious structures at the tops of trees, close to a stretch of water, and though one thinks of the heron as a solitary bird, I've counted as many as

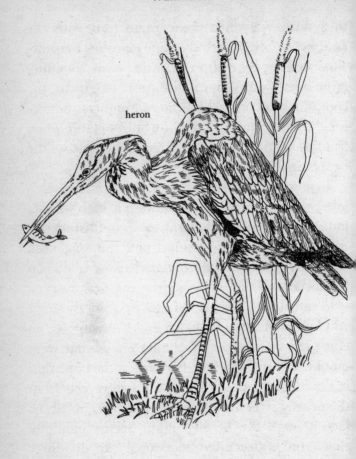

heron

thirty together at a local heronry in the breeding season, and I don't suppose that's exceptional.

All sorts of things appear on the heron's menu. Fish, eels and water-beetles in the ponds; crabs and prawns in tidal waters; mice, rats, grass-hoppers and small birds on land and, of course, the frog.

Chapter 5
OPEN WATER

Slimbridge is home to an enormous number and variety of ducks, many of which are exotic (of foreign extraction, and this book is not about them). But there are also all the native breeds of duck, which we can see in all the various 'wet' habitats of our country. Many could have swum quite happily in the preceding chapters, in the wetlands, in the rivers, and a few – the Eider, for example – in the sea.

But now I want to go to the areas of open water. Again we use lots of different names, usually depending on size, and 'pond' means a small area ('pool' even smaller). Larger stretches of water are often man-made, like reservoirs and flooded gravel-pits, and the really sizeable natural ones we call 'lakes', or 'lochs' in Scotland, or 'loughs' (different spelling, same pronunciation) in Ireland. 'Mere' is another name that's used, specially in the Lake District, and small hill-lakes are called 'tarns'.

The one bird that's associated particularly with all these sheets of open water is, for me, the duck, of which there are around fifteen native varieties. Generally we can divide them into two distinct types, the dabbling ducks and the diving ducks.

The dabbling ducks have two methods of feeding. At the water's edge or on the surface, they shove their beaks in shallowly, drawing water in at the front and squirting it out at the sides, to leave the seeds and insects that form part of their diet. The second method that dabbling ducks use is 'up-ending', when they tilt their bodies through ninety degrees to take food from the bottom or to feed on submerged waterweed. Dabbling ducks can dive if necessary (to avoid predators), but generally they dabble or up-end, reaching down, usually for between five and eight seconds, to different depths depending on their neck length. (Swans, which are also up-enders, can of course reach a long way down.)

Examples of dabbling ducks are Teal, Gadwall,

Pintail, Shoveler, Wigeon and Garganey, but far the commonest and best-known is the Mallard.

Often we refer to Mallard as 'wild duck', but this is confusing, partly because all the other species are wild, and partly because Mallard in particular have adopted two different lifestyles. Some are truly wild and wary birds of open water, but some have adapted to city parks and other places close to humans, where they behave as tamely as farmyard birds.

The Mallard is a good example of the general rule among ducks – as among so many birds – that the male is gaudy and the female is dowdy. The Mallard drake's basic colour is greyish, but he has a dark-brownish breast, a white collar like a parson, and a spectacularly glossy green head. In February and March when the springtime courtship rituals begin, he shakes and bobs that glossy head as he chases after potential mates. The Mallard duck is a discreet mottled brown, a colour that assures excellent camouflage when she's about the important business of her life, the sitting of her eggs, and the brooding, and later the care of her ducklings, all of which she undertakes alone.

Sometimes she makes a nest in a tree, a pollarded willow perhaps, and then, after hatching, the tiny ducklings jump straight down from the nest into the water below. They, like the young of many water-birds, are nidifugous (a word that derives from two Latin ones – *nidus* which means a nest, and *fugere*, to flee). What this means is that, thanks to a longer incubation period, ducklings are equipped to leave the nest as soon as they are hatched and to swim immediately. Unlike many birds who must bring food for quite some time to their helpless babies in a nest that is vulnerable to predators, the duck can take her young to food and can keep them away from land enemies on the safety of the water. She warns them of danger with a soft 'quot-quot' noise (though the Mallard duck does have a very loud quack, while the drake's note is quieter and higher-pitched). Both take off direct from the water.

The principal structural differences between the dabbling ducks and the diving ducks is that the latter have their feet set further back – for more efficient propulsion, especially under water – and generally have backs that are more rounded than the straight ones of the dabblers, and shorter tails, held lower. The setting of the feet makes them even more ungainly waddlers on land than the dabblers.

In the water, diving ducks usually give a little jump in the air before submerging, and they can

female mallard with ducklings

swim well underwater in their search for food. The two commonest types are the Tufted Duck and the Pochard.

Tufted Ducks are animal feeders, liking small crustaceans and water-snails and sometimes small fish. The drakes are black birds with white flanks; they have an elongated black crest hanging from

the backs of their heads like a pigtail. The ducks
are a very dark brown with a small topknot.

Pochards are mainly vegetarian, preferring
underwater vegetation, and again the drake –
greyish with a chestnut head and a black breast – is
showier than the drab female.

pochard jumping before submerging

Other sorts of diving ducks are Scaup, Scoters,
Long-tailed Ducks and, in the North, Eider. Again
the Eider Ducks are beautifully camouflaged, and
the drakes quite the reverse, being the only kind of
ducks that are white above and black below, and
very striking they are too. It is the eider-down from

their nests that is used for stuffing pillows and quilts.

Another quite different sort of water-bird (not to be confused with the diving ducks) that frequents reservoirs and lochs, is the diver. All three of the varieties that breed in these islands – the Great Northern Diver, the Black-throated Diver and the Red-throated Diver – catch fish by submerging from the surface, and they are even more exaggeratedly designed than the diving ducks, their big webs being set so far back that they are the poorest of walkers on dry land. Perhaps to remove the need for walking, they build their nests at the very edge of the lochan (little loch), which they then use as a landing-strip, stopping quickly on their underparts, and not needing, as swans and ducks do, to skid along the surface on their feet.

Two other birds of the lakes are the goosander and the red-breasted merganser. These are 'sawbills', having long slender bills with serrated edges to help them grasp the fish on which they feed and for which they dive like cormorants.

The creation of new gravel pits and reservoirs has been good news for a family of waterbirds called the grebes, that are exclusively aquatic, being expert divers but poor fliers. Grebes are distinguished from ducks by their pointed bills and 'tailless' appearance, but principally by having feet that are not webbed but 'lobed' (having flaps along the toes). Usually, too, they hold their necks quite erect, which ducks and divers only do if alarmed.

There are five types of grebe, and the commonest is the smallest one, the Little Grebe or Dabchick, which breeds on all sorts of fresh water – ponds, streams and reservoirs. They are quite hard to spot, tending to skulk in cover and, on the water, to dive a great deal.

The largest and most spectacular of these birds, with the longest necks, are the Great Crested Grebes, and they are the reverse of the shy Dabchick when engaged in their courting display. This involves a dramatic ballet on water, where the two birds meet breast to breast and beak to beak, the dark 'horns' of feathers and red-black frills about their heads raised, their bodies lifted so high that they literally dance upon the surface. Like the other grebes, the Great Crested builds a floating nest made of weed and rushes, and the young can be seen riding on the backs of the adults. This is not just for the joy-ride, but to keep them safe from their main predator – the pike.

I'm not a proper bird-watcher, just someone interested if something new comes along, and I

courting display of the great crested grebe

remember one special occasion when something did.

We were on our way to stay with some friends who lived close by the shores of Loch Ness (more about that later).

'Come via Loch Ashie,' they said in a letter, giving directions. 'There's a pair of Slavonian Grebes nesting there. It's pretty unlikely you'll see them but you never know your luck.'

We looked in the bird book. 'Small grebe with chestnut neck and flanks, a black head and golden "horns",' the book said (the winter plumage is quite different, but this was summertime).

Well, we stopped the car when we reached Loch Ashie (the road runs right by one side of it) and got out. As Scottish lochs go it's a small one, but, even so, big enough to make the chances of seeing a Slavonian Grebe highly remote, we thought. We stared at the expanse of cold dark water, its surface bare of any living thing. Then, like a leading actor making his entrance upon the stage, there swam solemnly out from the rushes at our feet a small bird with chestnut neck and flanks, a black head and golden 'horns'.

The Highlands of Scotland are now the home of a quite different type of bird, a raptor, that depends upon water not as an element in which to swim but in which to hunt for its prey – fish.

This is the osprey, a chocolate-and-white fish-hawk, fairly commonly distributed in Scandinavia and Eastern Europe but long absent from the British Isles, until 1958. In that year a pair of ospreys built an eyrie on top of a low Scots pine by the side of Loch Garten in the Forest of Abernethy in Strath Spey.

osprey

Now follows a story that shows only too clearly the two sides of man – preserver and destroyer.

The RSPB set a round-the-clock watch on that pine tree, but despite it, egg-stealers climbed it in the middle of the night, were spotted, and escaped. Two broken osprey eggs were found on the ground and in the nest were two hens' eggs, marked with brown boot-polish. The following year much stricter precautions were taken to protect the eyrie, using barbed-wire and electric alarms, and three young ospreys were duly raised.

The RSPB has stood sentry ever since, and by 1982 (the latest figures I have) forty young ospreys had flown from the Loch Garten eyrie and there were twenty-five other known Highland sites. The watch though must be unrelenting. In 1977 an egg collector got the only clutch of four eggs. What does he think, I wonder, as he gloats over them somewhere? To whom could he show them? Only another egg-collector, I suppose. The osprey dives for fish feet first, a spectacular sight, often from as high as a hundred feet (thirty metres), and on the pads of its feet are short spikes that help to hold its prey. Egg-stealers, I rather feel, should be dropped into the water from thirty metres too.

Chapter 6
THE POND

Frogs are among many creatures that find a pond an ideal habitat, partly because of the temperature of the water. Because a pond is a small area of shallow fresh water (as opposed to the large deep lake) the temperature is much the same, top and bottom.

Though not as common as they were, there are still a great many village ponds all over the country, often on the village green. Now they're just decorative and no one would dream of drinking out of them, but once they were the main source of water supply for villagers and their livestock. The horse-drawn water-cart would deliver supplies to outlying houses and cottages.

Village ponds had other uses too. People who had committed minor offences – like nicking their neighbour's cabbages, perhaps – were ducked in the pond. They were tied to a special ducking-stool and then dunked in the water while everyone (I expect) stood around and laughed themselves silly. But the village pond wasn't funny for a witch. Anyone suspected of being a witch was chucked into the middle of the pond. If she floated, she was guilty. If she sank, she was innocent, but by the time she'd done quite a lot of sinking I don't suppose she got much pleasure from the verdict. And don't think that sort of thing happened hundreds of years ago. The last reported 'swimming' of a witch was in 1880.

Wayside ponds were important for quite another reason in the days of horse-drawn traffic. In hot weather the wooden wheels dried out and shrank, and unless the wood was thoroughly soaked, which would make it swell, the iron tyre would fall off it. So the carter would drive horse and wagon into the pond and let them both stand there.

You won't see that happening today, but you'll still see the same sorts of dragonflies the old carter would have seen, skimming over the surface of a summer pond. There are two main families of dragonflies, the hawkers and the darters. The hawker female deposits her eggs in water-plants that are near or just below the surface. The darter female hovers close to the water and lets her eggs go like little bombs, which just break the surface. From the dragonfly egg (of either sort) hatches a nymph, which takes between one and three years to develop, and which catches its own underwater prey, ranging from waterfleas to small fish like the 3-spined stickleback. When the adult dragonfly is ready to emerge, the nymph takes up position on a twig or a stone or a plant, usually at night, so that its head is just clear of the water. The casing of the nymph splits and the adult emerges, and can take to the air after twelve hours.

A huge variety (200 species) of freshwater bugs live in ponds, and the largest is the water-boatman, growing up to half an inch in size. It's not buoyant enough to float so if it stops swimming, it sinks. Therefore it feeds on plants at the bottom of the pond, before resurfacing again for air.

Many fish lay their eggs in ponds, attaching them to vegetation or stones, but the stickleback actually builds a nest, made of fragments of weed glued together with a sticky secretion. The male builds the nest, and guards it fiercely once his mate has laid her eggs in it. Red rags are supposed to infuriate bulls (though in fact any bright colour will do), but anything red will send the male stickleback into a fury of attack.

Ponds are the places to find the amphibians. These animals get their name from the Greek word *amphibios*, which means 'leading a double life', for that's what they do, being equally at home on the land or in the water, to which they return to breed.

The amphibians were the first creatures to haul themselves out of the seas and begin to spend a part of their lives on the land. Some of them in due course evolved into the reptiles that, though cold-blooded like their amphibious ancestors, had one great advantage over them. They laid (and still lay) eggs with leathery or chalky shells which prevented them drying up in the sun, and so, unlike the amphibians that have to lay their eggs in water, could live a land-based life.

One reptile that you may see in an English pond (for it's an excellent swimmer) is the grass snake. It comes to the pond for good reasons – to eat frogs, newts, fish, tadpoles and, very occasionally, toads, in addition to its land-based quarry of young birds, mice, voles and shrews. If you do pick up a grass snake (and be careful it's not an adder, recognizable by its diamond-marked back-stripe), the chances are that you'll regret it, not because it will bite you – it won't. But it will use its anal glands to let off the most awful stink that'll make you most unpopular with your family.

The grass snake can also feign death in the face of danger. It lies with its mouth open and its tongue hanging out, looking half-witted. In mid-summer the female grass snake lays thirty to forty eggs, and incubates them in the warmth of a manure heap or compost heap. The adults are eaten by hedgehogs, badgers and by large birds.

Six different kinds of amphibians are found in our ponds. There's one sort of frog, two sorts of toad, and three sorts of newt. All show, in their progression from egg to adult, the same path from water to land that their ancestors followed. Frog tadpoles, toad tadpoles and newt larvae all begin life with gills to allow them to live underwater, and progress gradually to being able to breathe oxygen directly from the air.

Telling the three types of newt apart is not hard if you look carefully at them. To some extent it's a matter of size. The smallest sort (three inches [eight centimetres] long) is the Palmate Newt. Palmate means hand-shaped, and that's the clue. Have a look at the toes on the back feet and if they're webbed, it's a male Palmate Newt. What

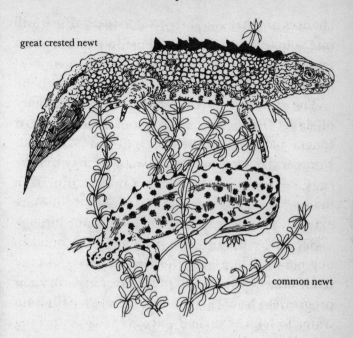

great crested newt

common newt

about the female, you say? Ah well, that's trickier because female Palmate Newts don't have webbed hindfeet and are very easy to confuse with female Common Newts. Now you must look at the throat and if it's spotted, it's a Common female, and if it's not spotted, it's a Palmate. Easy, did I say?

The next biggest (four inches [ten centimetres] long) is the Common or Smooth Newt, which is rather drab when it's on land; but in the springtime the males become quite showy, their light upper parts being spotted with black and their undersides red or orange, while they sport a crest along their backs and tails.

But the showiest of the three newts, and the largest (five inches [thirteen centimetres], sometimes six [fifteen]) is the Great or Warty Crested Newt. As the name tells you, this animal has a rough warty skin and a magnificent crest along back and tail, making it into a perfect miniature dragon. Nor are the females left out of the colourfulness, for both sexes have brilliant orange undersides peppered with black spots.

In all three varieties, the female lays eggs in the pond from April on till July, attaching each egg singly to the leaf of a water-plant and then bending the leaf over to protect the egg.

Newt tadpoles are not quite like frog and toad tadpoles, but are more like miniatures of their parents (though legless at first). In winter newts hibernate in holes in the ground, under stones or logs, or on occasion in the cellars of houses.

Toads hibernate too, in much the same places. A house in which my parents once lived had cellars that were groaning with toads of all sizes, though I've never been able to work out how the tiny ones, that were always in danger of being stepped on, got there from their birthplace; which again must have been a pond of some sort. Toads spawn deeper than frogs, laying their eggs in long strings (each string containing anything between 300 and 7,000 eggs) which they wrap round water-plants. Toad tadpoles are darker-backed than frog tadpoles, and take four years to mature into adults.

As well as the Common Toad, there is a rare variety of toad called the Natterjack, which is only found in certain areas like the Fens in East Anglia. There it's sometimes called the Running Toad, for it doesn't hop but runs. Frogs can make long athletic leaps, Common Toads content themselves with short awkward hops, but the Natterjack Toad runs like a mouse. It often hibernates in rabbit burrows.

Both the Natterjack and the Great Crested Newt are protected species incidentally. Because of the nature of the areas where they live, Natterjacks are forced to lay their eggs in sandy pools that are usually almost plantless, and therefore they can't anchor their egg-strings. Also, because sandy pools dry out fast in hot weather, the changing of the tadpoles into toadlets needs to be faster – six to eight weeks instead of the three months of the Common Toad's tadpoles.

The Common Toad eats insects, slugs, worms and snails, but it's interesting to note that they

common toad

only take moving prey. Anything that meets a toad and has the sense or luck to remain motionless, is ignored. The actual catching is done with the toad's forwardly fixed tongue which it rolls out. The victim is then drawn back into the toad's mouth and a curious thing happens. The toad actually draws its eyes down into its head, and the prey is squashed by the pressure between the tongue and the bottom of the eyeballs.

By the way, when the toad itself is confronted by

an enemy, it has a clever little dodge to discourage its possible attacker. It blows itself up, making its body seem much larger, and at the same time straightens its legs so that it seems to be standing on stilts.

Perhaps because the toad is slightly venomous, exuding a poison from the warts on its skin, it has always been disliked (most unfairly, I think) and thought of as a beast of the Devil or a familiar of witches. Fair play for toads, say I – I think they're lovely animals and I just wish one would adopt me and come and live permanently in my garden. And I'm sure they're bursting with brains. Certainly the man who wrote *The Wind in the Willows* thought so.

> The clever men at Oxford
> Know all that there is to be knowed
> But none of them know one half so much
> As intelligent Mr Toad.

And so to the frog. In springtime, specially on warm wet nights, mature frogs set out on a journey to a pond of their choice (sometimes the pond where they were once tadpoles), and very determined they are to get there, regardless of such dangers as road-crossing. There's a village not far from where I live that has on its flanks a large pond, to reach which frogs must cross the road. Every spring at the right time some thoughtful person puts a notice up at each end of the village, reading

CAUTION! FROGS CROSSING.

(I think they should put AND TOADS, because toads are always particularly eager to return to their birthplace.) But, even so, there are so many

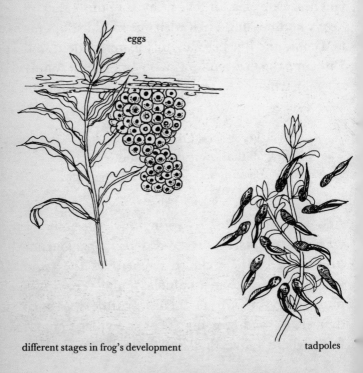

eggs

different stages in frog's development

tadpoles

frogs that would a-wooing go that there are always quite a lot of flattened corpses.

A female Common or Green Frog lays 1,000 (or even as many as 3,000) eggs in one batch, which form a kind of raft in jelly. The mass of eggs is far bigger than the parent, so how did they ever fit inside her? The answer is that when each egg was inside the mother's body, it was covered with a thin layer of slime; but once the eggs are laid and

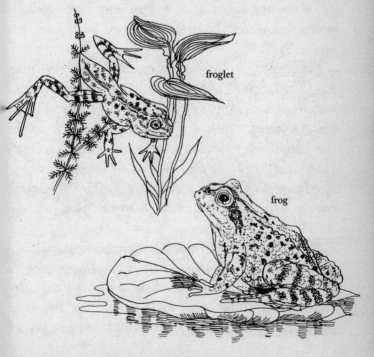

froglet

frog

come into contact with water, either rain or dew, the slime swells enormously. In days gone by country people, farmers or shepherds, found great lumps of whitish jelly lying on the ground. Being able to think of no explanation for this, they concluded that the stuff had fallen from the sky, and they called it Star-shine or Rot of the Stars. What had actually happened was that some predator, an otter perhaps, had eaten a lot of frogs, but had not been able to digest the jelly-producing glands in the frogs' bodies; so these were voided on to the ground and then swelled with dew or rain.

Froglets about to take to the land for the first time wait for a shower of rain and then emerge in large numbers. I saw this happen once as I was walking along a country road that was near a pond. I could see something moving across the road surface some way ahead of me, and when I got there, lo and behold, there was a great army of tiny froglets, hundreds and hundreds of them hopping across the tarmac.

Stories have been told of a 'rain' of frogs, when showers of them drop out of the skies, and in fact there is a possible explanation. Tornadoes can whip up the entire contents of a pond and deposit them on dry land, and it's recorded that in 1921 a number of streets in North London were literally carpeted with froglets.

When the female frog lays her egg-raft, it first sinks to the bottom of the pond, and then, as the jelly absorbs water, rises to the surface as the familiar frog-spawn. The tadpole begins life as a primitive creature with gills. Then at seven to eight weeks the hindlegs are fully developed and so are the lungs, which means that the tadpole must visit the surface. At three months it has become a froglet with a tail, and by midsummer the baby frogs, now perhaps half an inch long, are ready to leave their pond. But they must face a host of enemies. Insects, newts, fish and birds preyed on them while they were in the pond, but now the list is longer – herons, pike, grass snakes, rats, otters and hedgehogs. The number of frogs that survive to maturity at three years of age is but a tiny fraction of the original company of tadpoles.

To escape all these predators and to catch their own prey (snails, worms, insects and slugs, like the toad) frogs have to jump quickly. But they mustn't jump aimlessly when danger threatens, or it's out of the frying-pan into the fire. Colour plays a part in telling the frog where to jump. It generally prefers to jump towards a blue background rather than a green or yellow one, and because water transmits more blue light than the surrounding vegetation, this may take them into the safety of a pond.

Let's say goodbye to ponds with a poem I once saw. I don't know who wrote it but I've always rather liked it.

> What a wonderful bird the frog are.
> When he hop, he fly – almost.
> When he croak, he sing – almost.
> He ain't got any brains – hardly.
> > Anon.

Chapter 7
IN THE DEPTHS

One British lake – Loch Ness – may be the home of an animal as yet unknown to science. Indeed, many scientists still fall over backwards in their efforts to discredit the idea that what is popularly called the Loch Ness Monster could possibly exist.

As Gerald Durrell says (and he knows a bit about animals) in the preface to a book called *The Loch Ness Story* '. . . faced with evidence that seems to me incontrovertible . . . the scientific fraternity nervously take refuge behind a barricade of ripples, leaping salmon, shadows, dead stags, logs of wood, branches, and what must surely be the most agile and acrobatic strings of otters ever seen, rather than admit that there is something large, strange and unknown to science in the cold waters of the Loch.'

Durrell goes on to remark that people say that prehistoric monsters (as the newspapers loosely call them) could not possibly exist today. Yet in New Zealand there's a lizard-like creature called the tuatara, which has remained completely unchanged for two million years, and the example of the coelacanth is even more striking. In 1938 one of these five-foot-long, steel-blue-coloured fish was caught by a fishing-boat off Madagascar. Yet scientists had previously considered that the coelacanth had been extinct for between sixty and seventy million years!

Reports of something strange living in Loch Ness are not new. The first mention was by Saint Columba in 565 AD, the man who brought Christianity to Scotland. And ever since then there have been stories of the Kelpie or Water Horse, a monster animal that inhabited the loch. There were sightings at the end of the eighteenth century and during the nineteenth, but it was on the afternoon of 14 April 1933, when I was eleven years of age, that the first modern news of the Loch Ness Monster burst upon the world.

To be sure, the local press had reported sightings of an unidentified animal before this date, but

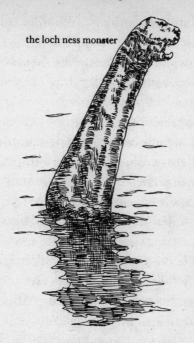

the loch ness monster

it was the account given by a Mr and Mrs John Mackay of Drumnadrochit that is traditionally credited with being the start of the saga of the monster. They saw – and watched for several minutes – 'an enormous animal rolling and plunging' in the centre of the loch, until it disappeared with a great upsurge of water.

Since then there have been many, many sightings by many, many people. A good number of still photographs have been taken, the most famous perhaps being the 'Surgeon's Photograph', taken in the spring of 1934 by a doctor named Wilson, which clearly shows the animal's raised head and neck emerging from the water. It is a better-defined and more compelling picture than many of the others, most of which, to be honest, are somewhat blurred and indistinct. Nevertheless, most of them show an object or objects that are difficult to explain except in terms of a large unknown creature.

More recently, cameras and sonar equipment have gone under the waters of the loch in their search, and their evidence is much more compelling. But still no one can say – with *absolute* certainty – that there are unknown creatures living in Loch Ness. No one has caught one alive. No one has seen a dead specimen, or a skeleton, or even a bit of skin. (No one knew, by the way, of the existence of that strange relative of the giraffe, the okapi, until in 1901 a bit of skin, thought to be from some sort of forest zebra, was brought back from 'darkest' Africa, and still some years passed before live specimens were found.) No one can say for sure what is in 'darkest' Loch Ness. You either believe in it or you don't.

Myself, I'm a believer, and not only because of such evidence as there is, from sightings, soundings, and on film, but because I know that everyone who lives near the loch will tell you unhesitatingly that the monster exists.

'Aye,' they say, 'they all think they're so smart down south, but we know the beasties are there, and that's all there is to it.'

Many of them, because they live by Loch Ness, have seen something themselves. Those friends of ours, that pointed us to the Slavonian Grebe on Loch Ashie, saw things not easy to explain, and the person for whom they worked has recorded a sighting that is typical of many. Her name was Lady Maud Baillie, the sister-in-law of former Prime Minister Harold Macmillan, and here's her description: 'I had just pointed out Urquhart Castle to the children' (she was with her grandsons) 'when one of them asked "Is that a rock out there?" I glanced across the water and saw something about one third of the way across the loch. I knew immediately that it could not be a rock that far out so I pulled the car into the side of the road. Just as I did so the "rock" moved off at a very rapid pace in a northerly direction and after a few seconds it was concealed by the roadside vegetation. We all hurried down to the water's edge but the object had gone. But it had left a terrific wash which soon hit the shore with some violence and caused one of the children to run back in horror . . .

Although none of us saw it for long enough to give any real details, we all saw two separate big dark humps in the water. There was no doubt that it was a very large living animal.'

One thing is certain: there's plenty of room in Loch Ness for large animals. From Fort William at the south end to Inverness at the north, it runs for twenty-four miles, the largest freshwater lake in Great Britain and the third deepest in Europe. It is comparatively narrow – up to one-and-a-half miles across. As for depth, in 1969 a miniature submarine went down to a depth of 820 feet (250 metres) and there recorded a maximum depth of 975 feet (297 metres).

Another certainty is that Loch Ness contains ample supplies of food for whatever may live in it. Its waters are fresh and unpolluted, and salmon and sea-trout migrate into it via the River Ness at the north end, on their way to ascend lochside rivers to their spawning-grounds. As well as these, the loch contains Brown Trout, huge shoals of Arctic Char and an enormous quantity of eels, some known to be quite large. So there's certainly plenty of grub for anyone with a taste for fish.

With 14,000 acres of surface water to look at, it's not surprising that countless people have stood and stared – as I often have – hoping against hope for a glimpse of the monster, but seeing only water, water and more water. There, I said 'monster' in the singular, still influenced by the stupid early idea that people had that there was just a single individual animal there; and what's more, thanks to cartoonists and silly picture-postcards and their own too vivid imagination, they pictured some kind of gigantic sea-serpent, with a dragon's head and umpteen serpentine coils. Some, I believe, still think like that.

But if there's one thing that's certain, it's that a species only survives by breeding, by replacing the old with the young, and that there must therefore be a colony of these creatures – whatever they may be – living in Loch Ness and feeding on its bountiful fish stocks. Common sense says they must be fish-eaters, and reports confirm this. For instance, a sighting in 1954 speaks of 'a big hump coming across the loch, salmon leaping out of its path, and the thing seeming to turn and follow the fish.'

Why then are the animals so elusive that, despite hundreds of thousands of hours of surface observation by thousands of monster-watchers, the results, in terms of photographic proof, have been so meagre? Because – and this is all we know of their habits – they are not primarily surface-dwellers, they are not inquisitive, and they most probably spend their time on the bottom and sides of the loch. How did they get there in the first place?

Either they've been trapped in it for thousands of years or they've entered more recently. Could there be an underground tunnel into the loch? No, for it is fifty-two feet (fifteen metres) above sea-level. Could they have come in through the River Ness? Well, the river is quite shallow and it seems unlikely that even young animals would have attempted to ascend it from the sea (though there have been sightings, in 1936 and 1965, of a fifteen-foot [four-and-a-half metre]-long humped body forging down to the sea – perhaps smaller specimens escaping?).

The trapping theory seems much more probable. When the last Ice Age ended about 10,000 years ago, the ice melted and the level of the sea was raised; many coastal valleys were thus flooded, until the land, freed of the weight of ice, slowly rose and separated the sea from the inland waters.

So – during this period when Loch Ness was linked to the sea – it's perfectly possible that a group of these animals swam into its sheltered waters and settled there. Eventually, as the land rose and Loch Ness became an enclosed lake, they found their return route to the sea blocked. Slowly the water lost its saltiness and the animals adapted to life in fresh water. Other species have certainly managed this change, for in parts of Africa there are sharks in freshwater lakes that were once connected to the sea.

What kind of animals could these be then, these left-behind creatures, almost certainly of very ancient extraction? Are they mammals? It doesn't seem so, for they would then need to come to the surface to breathe and surely there would have been many more sightings. Though it's possible, of course, that the nostrils may be set so high on the head that only a tiny bit of the creature would need to be exposed in all that area of often choppy water. Are they fish? It seems unlikely. All reports speak of a long neck, and of great size – ranging from an estimate of twenty to perhaps sixty feet (six to eighteen metres), far beyond the theoretical size of any gilled creature. Are they amphibians? Possibly, for there have been a number of reported sightings of and meetings with a huge unknown animal on the shores of the loch as it crossed the bordering road. Are they then reptiles?

This is the most generally held opinion – that the monsters of Loch Ness are most probably plesiosauruses. The plesiosaurus is a marine fish-eating

plesiosaurus

reptile, thought to have been extinct for about seventy million years (the same length of time, note, as the coelacanth). Certainly we know from skeletal remains that members of the plesiosaur family, very large animals with long slender necks, small heads, long tails and four flippers, did originally exist in the area of the British Isles.

All the best evidence we have points to something plesiosaur-like, from the Surgeon's Photograph and a remarkable fifty feet of 16mm film shot by a man named Tim Dinsdale in 1960, the most experienced and dedicated of monster-watchers, to the even more amazing work of an American called Bob Rines. In the summer of 1972 one of his underwater cameras took a picture showing the flipper and side of a large animal, and simultaneously a sonar device recorded the passage of two thirty-foot (nine-metre)-long animals.

To sum up, what now seems likely to many people is that in Loch Ness is a herd of animals, varying in size from perhaps fifteen to fifty feet (four-and-a-half to fifteen metres), each with a long slender neck, a small snake-like head, a reasonably heavy body, a long powerful tail and four, apparently diamond-shaped flippers.

OK, you say – they're living and breeding in the loch, these animals. Well, then they're dying too, aren't they? They're not immortal. Why no bodies? The answer is simple and seems believable. Because of the coldness and immense depth of the steep-sided loch, a body, when it expires, settles on the bottom and is slowly covered by mud and silt. The coldness slows down the chemical reactions that would normally generate gases in the body and bring it back up. It begins to sink, and soon encounters such water pressure that there is no way it can come back to the surface.

After Rines' work in 1972, no less an authority than Sir Peter Scott became convinced of the existence of these animals, and Scott and Rines together suggested a name for the monster, so that it could be added to the schedule of protected wildlife. They called it *Nessiteras Rhombopteryx*, from the Greek, meaning 'the wonder of Ness with the diamond fin'. (An anagram of Nessiteras Rhombopteryx, it was noted with glee by the newspapers, was 'Monster Hoax by Sir Peter S.'!) They failed to notice that another anagram is 'Yes, both pix are Monsters. R.' (for Rines). Scott believes in it and so do thousands of reputable witnesses, yet the men in the back rooms of the Natural History Museum still stick to tree trunks and dead cows and people 'seeing things'. I think that they *were* seeing things, real living hitherto-unknown animals, and one day we shall know for sure.

Whatever it is, it's big, and I wouldn't like to meet it on a dark night (or a sunny day). Long-distance swimmers sometimes tackle the length of Loch Ness. I often wonder if they heard the story of Mrs Hambro.

In 1932 there was an explosion on the boat in

which she was travelling with members of her family on the loch, close inshore by Glendoe boathouse. They all had to swim for it. The others made it. She disappeared.

Divers went down soon after to try to recover the woman's body. They went down to 150 feet (forty-five metres) but could see nothing because of the gloom of the peaty water. But it's said that they did not at all care for the work, and were desperately glad to be pulled out of the water.

It's easy to feel the hair on your neck bristle, even if you're just standing on the shore. Suppose the Water Horse came suddenly out of the loch at your very feet? I was imagining this one day, standing at the water's edge towards the north end of the loch, by Dores, while my three children, who were quite small at the time, played at the top of the little pebbled beach.

'The Monster!' I cried suddenly, turning and running towards them, waving my arms.

'Look out! The Monster's coming!' and they all ran, yelling.

But afterwards, when the children had finished punching and kicking me in their angry relief, I still thought to myself that nothing on earth would ever persuade me to go on a boat on Loch Ness.

I remembered the words of a man called Alex

Campbell, who used to be one of the loch Water Bailiffs.

'It was a beautiful summer day . . . and I was rowing my boat in the middle of the loch. Without any warning the boat started to heave underneath. It was terrifying. My dog was with me in the boat – an Airedale terrier – and he leapt from where he was in the stern sheets to lie, crouching and shivering, under my seat. I was really scared.'

I don't blame him.

Chapter 8

BACK TO THE SEASIDE

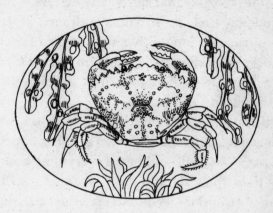

Let's go back to the sea. (After all, there's more water to watch there than anywhere else.)

We began by looking at the birds of the seaside but there are plenty of other animals, who live in the rock-pools and the caves, on the beaches and in the sea itself.

Exploring rock-pools is usually done in bare feet, and bare feet are vulnerable to a nip from a crab. Edible Crabs – the big red ones you see on the fishmonger's slab – live in the deep sea, but the one you're most likely to meet is the green Shore Crab. Crabs are the only animals that can scuttle sideways. They have five pairs of legs (the front pair being the strong pincers), and the end of each

hindleg is flattened, to form a paddle for swimming. They pull with one set of legs and push with
the other to make that sideways progress.

You may well find an empty crab shell. It will be
as wide as it is long – that's the mark of a Shore
Crab's shell, while the shell of an Edible Crab is
twice as wide as it is long. But an empty shell
doesn't mean a dead crab.

The problem that the growing crab has to deal
with is that, although its body is getting larger, its
carapace – its shell – is not. So everything becomes
very tight (just like you trying to wear your little
brother's trousers). What the crab does is to slough
off its old shell, and then wait for the new one
that it is wearing to stretch and harden.

Hermit Crabs deal with their growth troubles in
a different way. They have soft bodies, so to protect
themselves they squat inside empty shells. So
when a Hermit Crab feels that its lodging is no
longer roomy enough, it simply nips out of it and
finds itself a larger house. One claw is bigger than
the other, and with it the Hermit Crab blocks the
'door' of his new home. Sometimes a sea anemone
sits on top of it.

Sea anemones (of which there are about forty
different British species) are soft-bodied animals
that attach themselves to rocks or piers (where

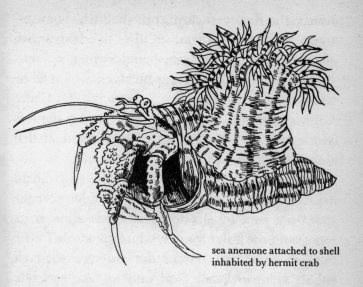

sea anemone attached to shell
inhabited by hermit crab

they themselves may be eaten by sea slugs). The
anemones are flesh-eating animals. When closed,
they look like blobs of jelly, when opened, like a
flower. But the petals of the flower are poisonous
tentacles. So a tiny shrimp, for example, is caught
by this 'flower', which then closes its petals; and
the doomed shrimp is eaten, the mouth of the sea
anemone being in the middle of the body. It can't
digest hard food, so presently the tentacles open
again and the mouth spits out the bits of the
shrimp shell.

The shells that you find on the beach – and very
fascinating and beautiful some of them are – are

simply the empty coverings of shellfish. Some of these shellfish are univalves, that live inside one permanent shell and move underwater on one 'foot', like a snail. Some are bivalves, which have two shells hinged together.

Two well-known bivalves are the fan-shaped cockles that live buried in soft wet sand in the low-water area of the beach, and the mussels that live on rocks and on the piles of piers. Mussels never move away from home; each is tethered to its spot on a rock by silken threads that allow it to move with the flow of water, which must run freely through the two parts of the mussel's shell to enable it to pick out food and to take in fresh oxygen. Other bivalves are razorshells, and scallops which move by clapping their two halves together.

Among the univalve shellfish are the periwinkle family (the Small, the Rough, the Flat, and the Common Periwinkle which is the one you eat), and the whelks, also called buckies, which cling to rocks. Other univalves are cowries (small in this country but in the tropics there are cowries as big as your hand), barnacles (which stick fast, often in vast numbers, to the bottoms of ships but do not give birth to geese!) and limpets.

The limpet has a very strong foot, and once the

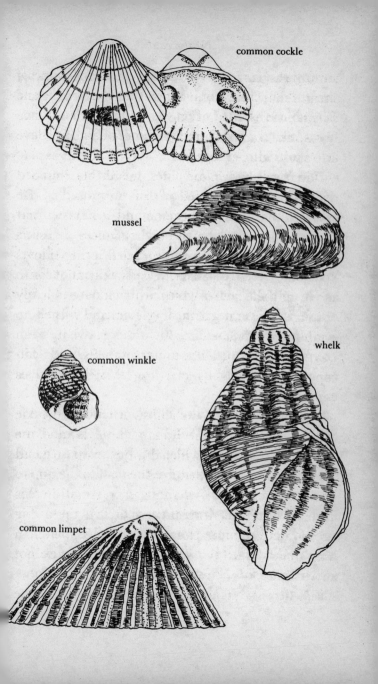

common cockle

mussel

common winkle

whelk

common limpet

sea covers it, it walks across the rocks eating minute short seaweeds. When the tide turns, each limpet returns to the exact spot from which it came.

It seems confusing that the times of high and low tide vary with each passing day, but the explanation is quite simple. 'Tides' mean the alternate rise and fall of the surface of the sea, caused by the gravitational pull of the moon and sun. When the moon and sun act together, this causes a higher high tide and a lower low tide (called spring-tides). When they act in opposition, the sea does not come as far up the beach or go so far back down (neap-tides). Spring or neap, the level rises and falls twice every lunar day, and as a lunar day is twenty-four hours and fifty minutes, tomorrow's high tide, for example, will be fifty minutes later than it was today.

Flat-fish that visit the shore for food are ocean fish, but the varieties found in rock-pools are more of the 'goldfish' type, like the blenny that darts very quickly from one side of the pool to the other, and the goby. The male goby scoops out a cave under a stone, in which the female lays up to 300 eggs. These the male guards faithfully, spending hours aerating the water round the eggs by swishing his fins. The goby has a sucker on its hind fins so that in rough water, when the tide comes in,

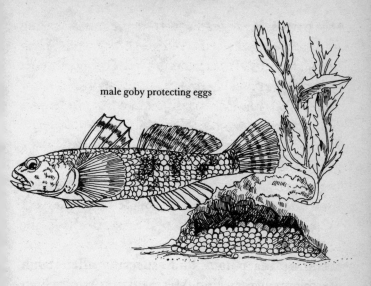

male goby protecting eggs

it can cling to a rock. Sticklebacks too inhabit rock-pools – not the 3-spined sort found in inland ponds, but the 15-spined marine variety.

Then there are prawns and shrimps. Size apart, you can distinguish one from the other for the prawn has a 'beak' between its two pairs of feelers (antennae), while the shrimp has no beak and only one pair of feelers.

Down on the wet sand you may find the Common Starfish which has four to six arms, and the Brittle Starfish (which lives up to its name, though all starfish can re-grow any arms they may lose). Something else you may come across is the sea

common starfish and lugworm casts on the sand

urchin or sea potato, and especially after rough weather you may find Mermaids' Purses, which are the egg-cases (one baby per purse) of skate and dogfish. Skate purses are black, those of dogfish brown.

Then there's the jellyfish. Jellyfish are nearly all water, and they dry up quickly in the sun when beached. Better not to touch them, for some are irritant. The jellyfish has frills and long trailing tentacles to catch its food. It swims by opening and closing its dome, just as you open and close an umbrella.

If you find dozens of string-like coils of wet sand and wonder what caused them, they mark the back end of the U-shaped burrows made by lugworms.

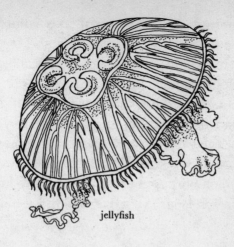

jellyfish

Lugworms obtain their food just as earthworms do, but instead of earth, they eat sand.

Beyond the sand is the sea, sometimes flat as a mill-pond, sometimes choppy with 'white horses' rearing their heads, sometimes rough with a heavy swell that sends breakers crashing on to the shore. On its surface you may see nothing much – a few gulls rocking, a cormorant flying low above the waves – but underneath the sea is teeming with life; flat-fish, herring, cod, bass, mackerel and countless other kinds.

One day you just might see a number of what look like huge fish – five to six feet in length – cartwheeling out of the water, some distance out if the weather is fair, but quite close inshore if (or so the fishermen say) bad weather is coming. But they are not fish. They are mammals, needing to surface to breathe. They are porpoises, a branch of the dolphin family, and are in fact one of the toothed whales. There are seven different sorts of porpoise worldwide, but the commonest – you'll be amazed to hear – is the Common Porpoise, often seen in small schools in British coastal waters.

Common porpoises are usually four to five-and-a-half feet in length (not over six-and-a-half), and

common porpoise

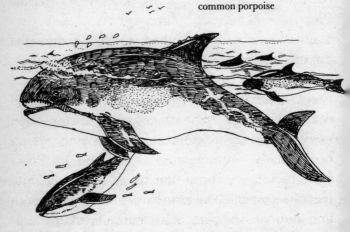

weigh on average 110 pounds (fifty kilograms). They have a blunt head, without the 'beak' of the dolphin.

Though they indulge in the cartwheeling motion (called 'porpoising') to take in air, they seem also to be very playful by nature, porpoising offshore or round boats just for the fun of it. Sometimes porpoises go up rivers and even reach inland lakes. When fishing – for squid and crustaceans, for cod, salmon or herrings (Devon folk call them ''errin 'ogs') – they submerge for up to five minutes.

The female porpoise has a single youngster around June, which grows fantastically quickly. Not surprising when you consider the richness of a porpoise's milk. Really rich (Jersey) cows' milk contains between five to six per cent butterfat. Porpoise milk has fifty per cent.

Porpoises are not hunted now, except for 'sportsmen' with rifles who like to kill them for fun. Cruel, eh? More of that in a minute.

A fish that is sometimes seen around the Cornish coast is the Basking Shark, a huge monster, often more than thirty feet (nine metres) long, which occasionally wanders into the shallows. Don't worry if you meet one – this is no Jaws. It is quite harmless and feeds on plankton (microscopic plant and animal life) which it strains from the seawater.

Another kind of shark that comes into our waters is the Porbeagle. Porbeagles, which have been recorded to ten feet (three metres) in length with a weight of five hundredweights, are found

basking shark

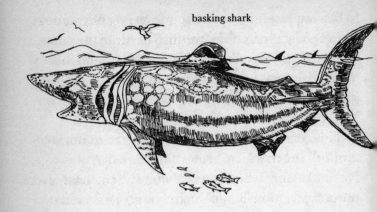

mainly off the Cornish coast, and feed on mackerel, cod, haddock and whiting. They have also been found in Pembrokeshire waters, as I can state with absolute certainty because my father and mother and their friends caught a number in the Caldey Roads off Tenby, fifty years ago.

The fishing method was very crude. First, catch some mackerel for bait. Then, attach half a mackerel to multiple hooks on a long length of strong weighted line and lower to the bottom. Drag behind a slow-moving boat, pulling in line gradually. When the Porbeagle takes the rising bait, pull like billy-o.

And they took some pulling in, too, for several of them were 150 pounds (sixty-eight kilograms) in weight. And they took some killing.

At the time it seemed to me very exciting and thrilling – the catching, the dispatching, the photographs of huge suspended fish and proud smiling anglers taken on the quayside; the teeth were pulled out for necklaces, the useless great body was fit only for manure.

Now, looking back, it seems barbaric. But who am I to say that?

At the age I then was, about fifteen, I fancied myself as a 'sportsman', and though I never fired a rifle at a porpoise, I used to shoot at cormorants from the boat with a shotgun. But one day I did something of which I am bitterly ashamed.

We'd been out early on a flat-calm morning, fishing for mackerel (few things taste better for breakfast than a mackerel you've just caught), and I had my gun in the boat with me, on the offchance of a pot at a cormorant. Suddenly we saw ahead of us a dorsal fin sticking out above the calm surface, stationary.

The boatman shut off the engine and we glided alongside and stopped.

'What is it?' someone said.

'It's a Sun-fish!' I said.

I had seen pictures of this extraordinary animal – short (its proper name is the Short Sun-fish) but massively built, blunt-ended, shaped just like a

sun-fish

huge beer-barrel. They grow to as much as eight feet (two-and-a-half metres) long and weigh one hundredweight for each foot of their length though, amazingly, the spinal cord of the Sun-fish, however large, is only one inch long. This one, I guess, was about six feet long, and it was asleep, for this is the habit of Sun-fish: to rise to the surface and doze, the dorsal fin sticking out.

Now, I can hardly believe what I did.

I pointed my gun at the huge barrel back and fired both barrels into it. There was a great gout of blood that stained the water all around, and the creature sank like a stone to its death.

I wondered whether or not to tell this story, because there are few things that I have done in my life that I'm less proud of, but I decided to, in the hope that it just might stop someone who reads this from killing something needlessly, cruelly, as I did.

As I've said before, if you feel that no one has the right to take the life of any animal, then you must become a vegetarian. Most of us condone the humane killing of creatures that are needed as food. But needless, pointless killing of any creature can never be excused.

If you should ever be tempted, remember the story of my Sun-fish.

I've left till last a favourite water-animal – the seal.

Legend has it that seals are the souls of all the sinful people for whom there was no room in Noah's Ark, condemned to float sadly in the seas for ever, and I suppose it's easy to imagine a melancholy look in the seal's big round eyes. But in fact people who have reared orphans and treated them as domestic pets, have found that they are happy and playful creatures and highly intelligent as well.

R. M. Lockley, the great Pembrokeshire naturalist, had a tame seal that was, he considered, at two months of age as intelligent as any housedog or indeed child of two years. Another tame seal learned twenty-four commands, including 'Wipe your nose' (with its flipper).

Around our shores there are two varieties of seal. The Grey Seal (which is not always grey) likes rocky shores, such as Pembrokeshire and Cornwall have to offer. The Common Seal (which is not all that common) prefers flat shores and mudbanks, and is found on the east coast, in the Wash, for example, and by the lochs of western Scotland. It isn't all that easy to tell the two types apart, but the Grey Seal is the larger, with a flatter longer head and a Roman nose, while the smaller Common Seal has a more dog-like head.

Seals are mammals whose evolution has equipped them for life in the sea; though they are not, like whales and dolphins, totally aquatic but can move (very clumsily) on land. The sea-lion, which has mobile hind-limbs, can progress by a shuffling waddle, but in seals, where the legs evolved into flippers, the rear limbs have become specialized and tail-like, and must be dragged along, either by

grey seals

rowing movements or sometimes by using one 'hand' after the other. Progress on land for a seal is pitifully slug-like, though they can go downhill quite fast.

In general, everything about the seal is adapted to a water-life. The tail is a mere stump, there are no external ear-flaps, and the body is beautifully streamlined for swimming; this it does by side-to-side movements of its hind-flippers, the fore-flippers being used for steering or slow swimming. To protect it from the cold, it has a coating of blubber up to seven centimetres (almost three inches) thick.

A mammal with lungs – as opposed to a fish with gills – the seal must come regularly to the surface to breathe. Usually they dive and remain submerged for between five and seven minutes. (Imagine holding your breath that long! But wait.) Maximum times have been recorded of fifteen minutes for a Common and twenty minutes for a Grey Seal, and a Weddell Seal of the Antarctic is known to have dived to a depth of 2000 feet (600 metres) and stayed down for forty minutes!

Seals are carnivores, eating all sorts of fish, squid and crustaceans and shellfish. Skate, ray and conger eel are much fancied. They don't need to drink fresh water, since sea-water doesn't hurt them and anyway they get most of their liquid needs from their food.

Underwater, ears and nostrils closed, they call to one another as they hunt, helped by their sensitive whiskers. The eyes see well below the surface, but it has been proved that blind seals can hunt perfectly efficiently and maintain themselves in the best of health.

Seals sleep at sea by one of two methods. Either they sink and rise again at about five minute intervals, or they sleep upright in the water, the nostrils just above the surface, which is called 'bottling'.

The seal cow has a single pup. Those of the Common Seal are born in the spring and must swim on the first returning tide after their entry into the world; to start with, they are not good at diving, so the mother tucks the baby under her flipper and down she goes.

Grey Seal pups are born in the autumn, pure white at first, and they stay on land until they take their first swim at about five weeks. The mother will wean her pup at three weeks, by which age it must have grown from a birthweight of around thirty-one pounds (fourteen kilograms) to about one hundred and ten pounds (fifty kilograms) or else it won't survive the winter. As with the porpoise, the seal's milk is immensely rich in butterfat.

The mammary glands of the seal cow are actually retractable; they distend at the touch of the calf's nose, and afterwards retract to prevent abrasion on land or in the sea; and the pup's tongue is notched at its tip, to get a firmer grip of the mother's small teat. It can suck on land, on water or underwater.

Common Seals, it is thought, may be able to give birth at sea (perhaps if prevented by foul weather from hauling out on to land). The just-born calf floats up to the surface, nostrils above water, where it either remains instinctively or is supported by the mother.

The cries that a large number of seals make have been described as 'singing', by Irish fishermen and others, but in fact the explanation for the noise is probably simpler. In a herd of seals hauled out to rest, on sandback, beach or reef, each adult will be separated from its neighbour by a distance equivalent to about two seal-body widths (say three to four feet). Any movement by that neighbour, even in sleep – the touch of a flipper perhaps – that breaches that personal territorial space will cause a noise of protest, and in a large herd this can swell to a chorus. Another supposed fact, in addition to singing, is that seals respond to music. Lockley tried this. He invited a company of people and brought his tame seal into the drawing-room, placing her backside on some sheets of newspaper (just in case). Then a lady flautist stood before the animal and began to play a haunting melody upon her flute.

Hardly had the soulful music of the woodwind begun when the seal replied, first with some very rude wind music of its own, and then by squirting an enormous mess on the newspapers.

We began in Pembrokeshire. Let's end off that coast, by the two main breeding islands of the Grey Seal in Welsh waters – Skomer and Ramsey Islands.

The words are those of Lockley, as he watches from a niche high in the cliffs above a sheltered bay. The day was calm and sunlit.

'The master bull lazily parted the smooth water, making a chevron of ripples as he patrolled the seaward edge of his territory. The three cows and their calves were all asleep, the calves on land, the cows under the shallow water.

The bull passed over the sleeping forms of the cows which from the height of my look-out on the cliff lay like pale silver-blue torpedoes at rest . . . Possibly they opened their eyes as the bull glided past . . . There was little more movement until well after noon. The cows, asleep under water, rose at regular intervals to breathe; through the telescope I could see their nostrils open and shut on an average a dozen times before each re-submergence. Even the bull seemed infected with the noon heat and the torpor of his women. He halted for long moments . . . lying horizontally with his back a shining oval in the sun and air. Occasionally he pivoted, so that his head pointed heavenwards, and for a while he floated upright, blinking peacefully.'

What a picture.

Chapter 9
SILVER BUBBLES

I hope I've left you with a few pictures.

Of a bridge perhaps, over a river in which trout lie, their noses pointed upstream, tails and fins fanning gently to hold their stations against the current. Maybe there's a dipper's nest under the curve of the stone arch through which a kingfisher suddenly blazes.

Or of a marshland perhaps, where the Grey Geese come flying in in their arrowheads, sounding for all the world like a pack of hounds baying in the sky.

Or a village pond, where the moorhens swim jerkily among the bulrushes, and the frogs come courting in the springtime.

Or maybe you'll see in your mind a great Atlantic cliff where the seabirds whirl and cry, and at its foot, riding easily in the swell, the Grey Seals with their round, whiskered, watching faces.

In *Country Watch*, the last animal I spoke of was a magpie, in *Town Watch* a sparrow, both birds, both common, successful, in no danger of being lost to us.

I think I'd like to end *Water Watch* with one last mention of a mammal that, for me, personifies the spirit of all water-creatures, moving as it does through river and brook and lake and pond and down to the sea itself – the otter.

How marvellous it would be if that scoreline that now applies in so much of England, 'Otters – o', could, thanks to legal protection and conservation measures and man's general goodwill, become a thing of the past. So that many of us, in the not too distant future, could stand on the bank of a stream and watch that long string of silver bubbles rising again through the clear water.

BIBLIOGRAPHY

The Sunday Times Countryside Companion, by Geoffrey Young (Country Life Books, 1985)

Grey Seal, Common Seal, by R. M. Lockley (André Deutsch Ltd, 1966)

Seals, by Robert Burton (The Bodley Head, 1978)

Otters, by Noel Simon (J. M. Dent & Sons Ltd, 1981)

Birdwatch round Britain, by Dougall & Axell (Collins, 1982)

The Seashore and Seashore Life (Ladybird Books, 1964)

Birdwatching in Inland Fresh Waters, by M. A. Ogilvie (Severn House Ltd, 1981)

Birdwatching on Estuaries, Coast and Sea, by Clare Lloyd (Severn House Ltd, 1981)

Birds of Britain and Europe, by Hammond & Everett (Pan Books, 1980)

The Observer's Book of Sea Fishes (Warne, 1958)

Mammals of the Sea, by R. M. Martin (B. T. Batsford Ltd, 1977)

The Pond, by Thompson, Coldrey & Bernard (Collins, 1984)

A Guide to the Birds of the Coast, by Gibson-Hill (Constable, 1949)

Eels, by Christopher Moriarty (David & Charles, 1978)

Ponds, their wildlife and upkeep, by Robert Burton (David & Charles, 1977)

British Naturalists' Association Guide to Ponds and Streams, by John Clegg (The Crowood Press, 1985)

Special Mention
The Loch Ness Story, by Nicholas Mitchell (Terence Dalton, 1974)

INDEX

ACKNOWLEDGEMENTS

The author and publishers gratefully acknowledge permission to reproduce copyright material in the form of extracts taken from the following poems or books:

'An Otter' and 'Pike' by Ted Hughes, reprinted by permission of Faber and Faber Ltd; a poem from *Exhumations* (Methuen Books 1966) by Christopher Isherwood, reprinted by permission of Curtis Brown Ltd for the Estate of Christopher Isherwood, copyright © 1966; *Grey Seal, Common Seal* by R. M. Lockley (1966), reprinted by permission of André Deutsch Ltd; introduction by Gerald Durrell to *The Loch Ness Story* by Nicholas Mitchell, reprinted by permission of Terence Dalton Ltd; extract from *Tarka the Otter* by Henry Williamson, 1927, published by the Putnam Publishing Group, New York.

Every effort has been made to trace copyright holders. The author and publishers would like to hear from any copyright holders not acknowledged.

COUNTRY WATCH
Dick King-Smith

Animal-watching can be fascinating and fun, if you know what to look out for and how best to observe it. As well as telling you what to look out for, this book is full of surprising facts about animals (did you know the tiny mole can burrow its way through thirty pounds of earth in an hour?) and Dick King-Smith has lots of marvellous stories to tell about his own encounters with animals over the years.

TOWN WATCH
Dick King-Smith

It's surprising how many wild animals there are to be seen in towns today, and this book is crammed with information about the many mammals, birds, insects and reptiles that live within the bounds of our towns and cities. From rubbish tip pests like rats and cockroaches to protected species such as owls and bats, Dick King-Smith provides a wealth of information and stories about urban wildlife.

CREEPY-CRAWLIES
Paul Temple

At last! All you could ever want to know about creepy-crawlies – spiders, worms, caterpillars, centipedes, tadpoles and many more extraordinary creatures. This amusing book is chock-full of amazing facts and fun things to do – build a wormery, create a beehive, spy on ponds with an underwater scope!

WATERSHIP DOWN
Richard Adams

One dim, moonlit night a small band of rabbits leave the comfort and safety of their warren, and set out on a long and dangerous journey. A dramatic and totally gripping bestseller.

GREYFRIARS BOBBY
Eleanor Atkinson

A touching, true story about the little Skye terrier who returned every night for fourteen years to the shepherd's grave in Greyfriars churchyard – so dearly had he loved his master.

THE SHEEP-PIG
Dick King-Smith

The wonderful story about the sheep-dog Fly who adopts Babe the piglet and trains him to be a sheep-pig!

LASSIE COME-HOME
Eric Knight

The classic heartwarming story of a dog and her devotion, who travels hundreds of miles so that she can meet a boy by the school-house gate and be faithful to her duty.

RABBIT HILL
Robert Lawson

'New folks' coming to the house on the hill make all the difference to the animal community already in residence and they all wonder how things will change.

THE OTTERS' TALE
Gavin Maxwell

The enchanting true story of Gavin Maxwell's life with the three otters he kept as pets and the enormous changes they brought to his life.

THE SONG OF PENTECOST
W. J. Corbett

Pentecost is the leader of a tribe of harvest mice who have to go on a perilous journey from their polluted wasteland home to a new place to settle in the hills. A marvellously witty and exciting adventure story with intrepid heroes and deceptively charming villains.

JOE AND THE GLADIATOR
Catherine Cookson

How do you manage to look after a horse if you've no home or money? This is Joe's problem.

JOCK OF THE BUSHVELD
Sir Percy FitzPatrick

A classic tale of the Transvaal, told through the life and times of a bull terrier and his master.

THE WIND IN THE WILLOWS
Kenneth Grahame

The classic story of the riverbank adventures of Mole, Water Rat, Badger and Toad now freshly interpreted by one of England's finest contemporary illustrators, John Burningham.

JET, A GIFT TO THE FAMILY
Geoffrey Kilner

Who would have believed that a tiny, spindly, jet-black puppy was to lead the Reynolds family into the exciting world of greyhound racing? This perceptive and entertaining novel is about how Jet turns out to be a truly exceptional dog.

SOUNDER

William H. Armstrong

Sounder wasn't much to look at, half bulldog, half hound, but his voice was a glory, and so was his faithfulness. But these could not help his young owner against the cruelty and indifference of the men who take away his father's liberty. A tragic and compelling tale of fortitude and courage.

THE MOUSE AND HIS CHILD

Russell Hoban

The epic journey of the father mouse and his child from the toyshop to their eventual home.

A DOG CALLED NELSON

Bill Naughton

A real-life story about a one-eyed mongrel of remarkable character called Nelson. A lively, humorous and touching tale.

MRS FRISBY AND THE RATS OF NIMH

Robert C. O'Brien

A fabulous adventure about the mysterious, ultra-intelligent rats, their past and their secret connection with Mrs Frisby's late husband.

CHARLOTTE'S WEB

E. B. White

The tale of how a little girl called Fern, with the help of a friendly spider, manages to save her beloved pig Wilbur from the usual fate of nice fat little pigs.

TARKA THE OTTER

Henry Williamson

The classic tale of an otter's life and death in Devon is as true as a man's account of a wild animal can possibly be. This book was hailed as a masterpiece when first published and today Tarka is one of the best-loved creatures in world literature.